Web: zainacademy.us

mzain.org

Email: help@zainacademy.us

help@mzain.org

WhatsApp (Messaging & Call): +92 311 222 4261

International Call: +92 311 222 4261

US & Canada Call: +1 646 979 0865

Facebook: https://www.facebook.com/zainacademy

YouTube: https://www.youtube.com/c/zainacademy

LinkedIn: https://www.linkedin.com/in/mzainhabib/

Twitter: https://twitter.com/mzaincpacmacia

Instagram: https://www.instagram.com/mzain.cpa.cma.cia/

Pinterest: https://www.pinterest.com/mzainhabib/

Amazon: https://www.amazon.com/MUHAMMAD-ZAIN/e/B07K2G2R8M

Telegram: https://t.me/ZainAcademy

Tumblr: http://zainacademy.tumblr.com/

Medium: https://medium.com/@muhammad_zain_cpa_cma_cia

INDEX

LET'S CONNECT WITH EACH OTHER..01

PREFACE...03

CERTIFIED INTERNAL AUDITOR (CIA) – US BASIC INFORMATION.............................04

LETTER FROM MUHAMMAD ZAIN...16

SECTION A – FOUNDATIONS OF INTERNAL AUDITING – STUDY POINTS..................20

SECTION A – FOUNDATIONS OF INTERNAL AUDITING – TRUE / FALSE QUESTIONS.........................43

SECTION B – INDEPENDENCE AND OBJECTIVITY – STUDY POINTS...........................53

SECTION B – INDEPENDENCE AND OBJECTIVITY – TRUE / FALSE QUESTIONS..................61

SECTION C – PROFICIENCY AND DUE PROFESSIONAL CARE – STUDY POINTS.........65

SECTION C – PROFICIENCY AND DUE PROFESSIONAL CARE – TRUE / FALSE QUESTIONS.................73

SECTION D – QUALITY ASSURANCE AND IMPROVEMENT PROGRAM – STUDY POINTS.......79

SECTION D – QUALITY ASSURANCE AND IMPROVEMENT PROGRAM – TRUE / FALSE QUESTION...89

SECTION E – GOVERNANCE, RISK MANAGEMENT, AND CONTROL – STUDY POINTS.........99

SECTION E – GOVERNANCE, RISK MANAGEMENT AND CONTROL – TRUE / FALSE QUESTIONS....138

SECTION F – FRAUD RISKS – STUDY POINTS...147

SECTION F – FRAUD RISKS – TRUE / FALSE QUESTIONS...160

BOOKS WRITTEN BY MUHAMMAD ZAIN...165

QUOTES THAT WILL CHANGE YOUR LIFE..171

PREFACE

All the knowledge possessed by me is a gift from Almighty Allah. The Creator of the Heavens and the earth blessed me with the success of passing Certified Public Accountant (CPA), Certified Management Accountant (CMA), Certified Internal Auditor (CIA), and Masters of Business Administration (MBA) exams in 1st attempt. I am profoundly grateful to my family for providing all the resources and time at their disposal for my enrichment morally, physically, and spiritually. I am also thankful to my teachers, who delivered their knowledge, wisdom, and experience.

The knowledge, resources, views, facts, and information presented in this book are a voice from my heart bestowed by Allah and my experience gained during my entire lifetime. I capitalized hours searching the Internet, Blogs, Social media, and Wikipedia to update my knowledge and notebook as part of my continuous learning objective. I am highly indebted to contributors to Google, Blogs, Social Media, and Wikipedia for presenting me with the ocean of knowledge and insights. The more I dived deep into the ocean, the more I concluded that we human beings are only given limited knowledge, which is unexplored and undiscovered entirely to this date. This curiosity of mankind is bringing innovations, discoveries, and ideas. Any resemblance to any copyrighted material available on the planet is purely coincidental and unintentional. I allow the readers of this book to use it for any related educational purpose and reproduce the contents as long as the original text in this book is unaltered. I give reasonable assurance that the information provided in this book is correct according to my knowledge and belief. There may be circumstances where potential readers challenge the information presented. I welcome these challenges to correct me for future updates.

May the Lord, Master of the day of Judgement and to whom the sovereignty belongs, bless me more and my readers in this world and in particular in life hereafter (Ameen).

Muhammad Zain

CERTIFIED INTERNAL AUDITOR (CIA) - US BASIC INFORMATION

Certified Internal Auditor (CIA) certification is offered by the Institute of Internal Auditors (IIA), US. It is a premium internal auditing qualification having a global presence. CIA is a symbol of excellence in compliance reporting, risk management, and consultancy. CIA has three parts. Part 1 is known as Essentials of Internal Auditing, Part 2 is known as Practice of Internal Auditing, and Part 3 is known as Business Knowledge for Internal Auditing.

Zain Academy's purpose is to create the best CIA Exam Prep materials at affordable pricing.

The IIA releases the profession's primary guidance, such as the International Professional Practices Framework (IPPF), Code of Ethics, International Standards for the Professional Practice of Internal Auditing. Membership with IIA is not required to earn a CIA designation. Candidates can save their earned money by not choosing the membership.

Chapters and affiliated institutes hold regular meetings, seminars, and conferences to develop networking, contacts, and social bonding. It is advisable to attend these types of events to learn about the current practices in internal auditing.

Why Choose CIA

The Certified Internal Auditor (CIA) credential offers many benefits. CIA certification can help you move forward in a focused direction. CIA certification gives a message that you are a proficient internal auditor who can bring valuable insights and experience. CIA holders can be entrusted with significant responsibility. CIA also helps in increasing accounting knowledge and skill.

CIA holders earning potential is excellent as compared to non-certified peers. Companies retain talented individuals by giving them market-based remuneration, bonuses, perks, fringe benefits, vacations. Qualified individuals earning is multiplied if he/she opens consultancy, compliance or internal auditing firm. CIA certified deserves the respect of the peers.

Muhammad Zain

Way To Achieve CIA Credential

The candidates must meet the four Es requirements, i.e., Education, Ethics, Examination, and Experience for achieving the CIA designation. Three years is provided by the Institute to get certified. However, the candidates can apply for one of the three types of 1-year eligibility extension, i.e., hardship, non-hardship, and exam eligibility. Each type of extension has its procedures and fees. Please refer to the CIA Candidate Handbook as available from the IIA website.

Education – At least a Bachelor's degree from an accredited college or university. If the candidates do not have a bachelor's degree, then a verifiable seven years of internal auditing experience can be accepted.

Ethics – Reflect high moral and professional character and agree to abide by the IIA's Code of Ethics. Submit a Character Reference Form signed by a CIA certified or supervisor or professor.

Examination – This is the most important of all the requirements. Candidates spend considerable time clearing the three parts of the CIA exam.

Experience – Bachelor's degree holder has to demonstrate two years of working experience. However, the requirement is reduced to one year if the candidate is a Master's degree holder. The candidates can fulfill experience requirements even after passing the CIA exams. The experience gained can be in the accounting, finance, or internal audit department.

CIA Examination

Candidates have to pass three parts to become certified. If a candidate cannot pass all three parts within three years' time period, then the candidate will lose the credit for any part passed and will have to apply again to the Institute. The table is necessary to become familiar with the CIA structure.

Part	Title	MCQs	Time
1	Essentials of Internal Auditing	125	2.5 hours (150 mins)
2	Practice of Internal Auditing	100	2 hours (120 mins)
3	Business Knowledge for Internal Auditing	100	2 hours (120 mins)

IIA Retired Questions

Test Bank Questions available with all the publishers are retired questions by IIA. 75% of the questions are the same with every publisher. The rest, 25%, is their creativity.

REMEMBER that actual CIA exam questions are non-disclosed and are not available to anyone.

CIA Exam Scoring

The CIA exam is computer-graded. The candidate will receive the result within five minutes of finishing the exam. Scores are determined by the difficulty level of questions asked and converting the value of questions answered correctly to a scale that ranges between 250 to 750. A score of at least 600 is required to pass the exam, i.e., 80%. If the questions are of higher IQ level, the passing score can go below 600, but if the items tested are easy, then passing criteria can go up from 600.

Whether the questions being asked are easy or difficult, I suggest you target achieving an overall 85% in exams by accurately attempting the 107 correct questions out of 125 questions in CIA Part 1.

The trend analysis for several years of CIA exam passing ratio is between 40% to 44%.

Muhammad Zain

CIA Exam Dates

CIA exam can be taken at any day and time of your choice subject to two conditions:

- The day must be a normal working day except for weekends and public holidays; and
- The time of the exam must be within regular working hours.

It is highly recommended to select your exam date and time as early as possible to get the preferred appointment.

Documents Required By IIA

The following documents are required by the Institute when a candidate makes a profile at the Certification Candidate Management System (CCMS):

i.   A soft copy of an unexpired official passport or national candidate ID card;
ii. A soft copy of degree and transcripts;
iii. A soft copy of the character reference form duly attested;
iv. A soft copy of the experience reference form verified by a CIA or supervisor.

Once the candidate registers for an exam part and gets the authorization to test email from IIA, he has 180 days to schedule and sit for the exam. This email from IIA must be printed and carried by the candidate when he takes his exam.

Pearson VUE www.pearsonvue.com/iia conducts CIA examinations globally. Select the testing center location that is easily reachable for you.

Investment in CIA

Investment in the CIA is one time if the candidates pass all three parts in the first attempt. Investment in the CIA is advantageous throughout life.

CIA exam fee is presented in the following table.

S.No	Description	Member	Non-Member	Student
1.	Application fee	$ 115	$ 230	$ 65
2.	Part 1 fee	$ 280	$ 395	$ 230
3.	Part 2 fee	$ 230	$ 345	$ 180
4.	Part 3 fee	$ 230	$ 345	$ 180
	TOTAL	**$ 855**	**$ 1,315**	**$ 655**

I highly recommend the candidates pay their dues through **DEBIT CARD** only. This way, you will be free from all claims of the bank and will be much relieved. The target must be to clear the exams in 1st Attempt so that the examination fee is paid only once, and benefits of opportunity costs can be derived.

Investment in study materials, test bank questions, and lecture videos are separate and vary according to the candidate's preferences and study methods.

REMEMBER to subscribe to the study materials and test bank questions that are economical, comprehensive, updated, and excellent.

ALSO, REMEMBER to subscribe for each part separately to get the time benefit.

CIA Parts Selection Order

I recommend the candidates to begin their preparation with Part 1 first and then moving to Part 2 and Part 3. The candidates can pass all three parts easily in seven months.

Difficulty Level of CIA Part 1

CIA Part 1 is the foundation of all three parts. CIA Part 1 exam can be passed **quickly** if the candidates can exhibit the traits of Excellency, Creativity, Passionate, and Patience in their preparation and, in particular, on exam day.

The Candidates must have a clear vision of their future. They must be able to define their purpose of life. The will to win, the desire to succeed, the urge to reach full potential – these are the keys that will unlock the door of CIA certification.

The reason that many candidates find it difficult to achieve the CIA is that they are not able to define their goals or ever seriously consider them as believable or achievable. Champions can tell you where they are going, what they plan to do along the way, and with whom they will be sharing their adventure.

Keep looking for creativity, and don't settle for the less. You have that potential. It is just a matter of time that you explore and discover yourself. Once you find yourself and your capability, you will never be the same again.

CIA Part 1 – Syllabus

There are six sections in CIA Part 1.

a. Section A – Foundations of Internal Auditing – 15% weightage

b. Section B – Independence and Objectivity – 15% weightage

c. Section C – Proficiency and Due Professional Care – 18% weightage

d. Section D – Quality Assurance and Improvement Program – 7% weightage

e. Section E – Governance, Risk Management and Control – 35%

f. Section F – Fraud Risks – 10% weightage

Muhammad Zain

CIA Part 1 Preparation Time

It is generally observed that many of the CIA candidates are working executives. They have to allocate time for work, family, studies, and personal leisure. The candidates are ready for Part 1 exam if they can give at least 3 hours on weekdays and at least 6 hours on weekends for two months continuously.

The candidates must follow the steps to understand the concepts being part of the syllabus of CIA Part 1.

a. Read a whole particular section from the study book first with the questioning mind approach. Mark or highlight only the important paras or sentences in the book.

b. Attempt the True / False Questions of that particular section presented in the book to clarify the already read topics.

c. Attempt the Multiple Choice Questions of that particular section from the Test Bank without any time constraints. Focus must be on selecting the correct answers in the first place.

If you attempt any question correctly, proceed to the next question. These questions do not need to be reviewed ever again because a question once attempted successfully will always be correct in the future.

If any question attempted is wrong in the 1ˢᵗ place, mark or highlight or flag those questions. Furthermore, there might be instances in which you have selected the correct answer, but you doubt the result's outcome if attempted later. These questions also need to be marked or highlighted. These marked questions will form the basis of review, revision, and rehearsal at a later stage.

d. Read the explanation of the incorrect answers selected and try to understand the logic of the question and correct answer explanation.

Muhammad Zain

e. As you complete 80% of the total questions of a particular section, move to the next section, and repeat the steps from (a) to (d).

f. Revision of the already learned topics every week is warranted. Dedicate a particular day in a week in which you will only revise the already learned topics. Read only those paras from the book which have been highlighted. Attempt only those questions from Test Bank Questions, which have been marked or highlighted. Time Management must come into effect while re-attempting the questions. Each MCQ has to be attempted in 1.1 minutes. This way, you will revise the entire section smartly, and your anxiety level will decrease.

g. As you complete all the sections of the CIA Part 1, then focus on completing 100% of the MCQs from the Test Bank Questions.

   REMEMBER that each topic has an equal chance of selection in the exam. So you have to be prepared for every concept.

   ALSO REMEMBER that CIA Exams are of continuous 2.5 hour duration. Train your mind to be active for at least 3 hours during MCQs preparation.

The candidates must have updated study materials and test bank questions. The study materials must be simple, concise, and easy to understand. The majority of finance graduates and working executives prefer self-studies. Select test bank questions of any comprehensive publisher. Subscribing for more than one publisher's test bank questions will not help as most of the questions will be repetitive.

Video Lectures are of great aid. They increase the retention power of the candidates by at least 25%. Furthermore, the candidates can view them later at their ease and convenience. Many of the candidates prefer live classes or online interactive sessions. This can also increase the odds in your favor exponentially.

Muhammad Zain

Recommended Study Approach

CIA exams are computer-based. It is recommended that all your preparation, highlighting, and practice must be on the computer or laptop. The candidates must avoid the traditional method of studying and making notes via pen and paper. Pen and paper shall be used only for calculation-related purposes while attempting the test bank questions.

The candidates can study at any time of day or night, but my preferable time is an early morning daily at 4:30 am. This is the time where the human brain is at a high energy level. This is also the time of great silence.

You will be provided with earplugs in the center and must use them to avoid distractions from other candidates' noise. Silence also has its voice, which you will agree with me on your exam day. Your mind needs to be accustomed to it. Therefore, use good quality foam-based earplugs from day 1 of your preparation. You can find these earplugs from your local pharmacy.

You will be provided with black pens at the center and two sheets. Start using a black pen from day 1. Your mind must be able to recognize and work in a black pen.

Please become familiar with the MCQ screens and navigation of the Pearson VUE Testing Environment before the exams. The tour can be arranged from your computer. This will make you comfortable on your exam day.

How to Answer the MCQs in preparation and exams?

My preferable way of approaching any MCQ is provided below. Ask yourself three bold phrases in every MCQ.

a. **What are the requirements of the question?** The question's requirements are generally presented in the second last, or last line of the question. Read it thoroughly and then reread the whole question to filter out the extra information.

b. **What is the answer?** Read twice the answer choices carefully and then select the best answer. Numerical questions require double-checking of formulas and calculations.

c. **If you do not know the answer, make an educated guess.** The educated guess is a technique to filter out the two options out of four based on your insights. Now the two options are left to be paid attention to. Read the requirements of the question again and then the remaining two answer choices. Select the best one. This way, you will increase your odds in favor by 50%.

Attempt all the exam questions even if the testlet is more challenging, and time management is crucial. You will not be penalized for any incorrect choices being made. Your score is determined out of correct questions only. Mark or Flag all those questions which you want to review in end if the time allows.

Pearson VUE Testing Site Visit

After you schedule your appointment with Pearson VUE, visit the center at least three days before the exam to become familiar with the location. If the center is in a building, make yourself familiar with the security perimeters of the building as well. Make contingency plans to reach the exam center in case of any unexpected circumstances. Double-check the weather conditions in advance of the exam day.

Day Before Exam Day

This day is also vital in the candidate's life. Leave all the review, revisions, or attempting the test bank questions at least 24 hours before the exam day. CIA is a professional paper, and the candidate has to be ready at any time. You have done enough preparation. Trust in Allah and have confidence in your abilities. You have done enough training. It is now time to showcase your talent.

You will be intimidated to see the materials or revise the test bank questions or watch the lecture videos. Keep aside all these urges. Divert your mind to the most enjoyable activity. That enjoyable activity can be praying, meditating, walking in the garden, or even watching a good movie. Arrange all the required documents, clothes, shoes, calculators, funds, and other items in advance. Charge your cell phone if you plan to travel and navigate by Apps. The Mobile Data Connection package must be active. Sleep for at least 10 hours at night before the exam day.

Activities on Exam Day

- Take a good shower and wear comfortable clothing according to the weather conditions.

- Have a comprehensive meal that is easily digestible and consume any necessary medicines.

- Bring printouts of Authorization Letter / Confirmation Letter / Notice to Schedule received through email from Pearson VUE and Institute, mentioning candidate's name, section part, exam date, time, and venue.

- Two original forms of non-expired identification with photograph and signature are required. Therefore, bring an unexpired and signed passport and national identity card / driver's license along with you.

- Reach the exam center at least 60 minutes' prior of your appointment time.

- Drink coffee or tea before the exam so that you are charged enough.

- Visit the washroom before the start of exam.

- The mobile phone has to be switched off and placed in a locker along with wallets.

- You will not be given any complimentary breaks during the 2-hour exam. However, you can take one for taking a slight break for recharging yourself, visiting the washroom, and having water. However, the clock will continue to run.

- Do not make noise or stand up from the seat without permission. Raise your hand first. The invigilator will visit you, and then you can ask for pens, extra sheets for working or taking a break, or any malfunction encountered in exams.

- Once you finish your exam, review the mark or flagged questions and try to attempt in the remaining time. Your score is based on the number of questions you answer correctly. You are not penalized for selecting the wrong answer.

- Make sure to submit your exam and watch for the system's incoming message for acknowledging your submitted questions.

What To Do after Passing CIA Exams

Hats off to you for passing all three parts. Meet all other program requirements and complete the Certificate Order Form by logging into CCMS to get your certificate.

LETTER FROM MUHAMMAD ZAIN

21 October 2021

Dear **CIAs**,

السلام عليكم

peace be upon you

May Peace, Blessings, and Mercy of Allah be upon you and, in particular, on the Noble Messenger Prophet Muhammad (Peace Be Upon Him), his Family, and his Companions.

Be a symbol of excellence in your life. Always dream big and think beyond the dimensions of the Universe. Man is made to conquer the seven Heavens. Explore the purpose of your existence and discover the enormous potential that is within oneself. Having faith and trust in Creator will give you the light in the darkness and unchartered territories. There is always a silver lining beneath the dark skies. A creative mindset makes life simple. Work on your passion by synchronizing your soul, heart, and mind. We all will die one day, but only a few dare to live the life they wish for.

The Creator has created the entire Universe in six days. There is a great potential to discover the magnificent beauty that remains unexplored to date. This is only possible by seeking knowledge and applying them in our daily lives.

We are witnessing a moment in time that humanity has not ever experienced before. This is the digital transformation age. Artificial Intelligence, Blockchain Technology, Cryptocurrency, Business Intelligence, and Big Data are business norms.

Muhammad Zain

All the information is available in the blink of an eye. Whatever we think in mind comes in front of our screens. These advancements will change the dynamics of the whole world we live in today. All the traditional and so-called "modern" methods of doing work will be replaced by cloud computing. The work of accountants, doctors, engineers, pilots will no longer exist. The irredeemable paper money will be replaced by electronic money. Central Governments will only exist in name only. Universal Government and a unified taxation system will emerge. Virtual reality will be ordinary. Blind will be able to see, deaf will be able to hear, without limbs persons will be able to run, and mentally disabled people will utilize the maximum brain capacity through mental chip implants. Teleportation of humans will be done in a blink of an eye.

My advice to all readers around the world to focus on <u>entrepreneurship</u> after the certification. This is the only way of survival. Only those businesses are operational who have inelastic demand for their products or services and who are on cloud computing / virtual workplaces. Furthermore, invest surplus funds in real assets such as Gold, Silver, and property. They are the effective hedges against inflation and devaluation. They generate positive returns even in times of economic distress.

I highly recommend that my potential readers pay their interest-bearing debt at the earliest to avoid the debt trap and never go for this easy money for the foreseeable future, even in the form of credit cards. These are all the means to enslave the human race. Always spend out of your realized income. Save some funds for your family as a contingency measure.

Allow me the opportunity to present to you the **2022** edition of *Certified Internal Auditor (CIA) Part 1 Essentials of Internal Auditing* Study Book. This Study Book covers all the essential and relevant concepts and topics that will be tested in the CIA exams. It also includes the True / False questions to reinforce the core concepts. After reading this book, you will feel the difference. The practice of Test Bank Questions is essential from CIA Part 1 Test Bank Questions 2022 available from the Zain Academy website.

This Study Book can also be used by any person who wishes to become familiar with accounting, finance, and management topics. However, extreme care is required when rendering professional advice to clients.

Study with complete dedication and commitment. Make the goal of learning something new and different each day. Replace your fear with curiosity.

Let's work together towards the common goal of earning a Certified Internal Auditor (CIA) credential. My support and guidance will be with you TILL YOU PASS THE EXAMS. Furthermore, you can ask as many questions as you wish to either through WhatsApp or email, and I will answer to the best of my ability.

Your work is going to fill a large part of your life and the only way to be truly satisfied is to do what you believe is great work. The only way to do great work is to love what you do. If you haven't found it yet, keep looking. Don't settle. As with all matters of the heart, you will know when you find it.

Have the courage to follow your heart and intuition. They somehow already know what you truly want to become. Everything else is secondary.

Your imagination is everything. It is the preview of life's coming attractions. Only those who believe anything is possible can achieve things most would consider impossible.

Don't let the noise of others' opinions drown out your own inner voice.

Remembering that you are going to die is the best way I know to avoid the trap of thinking you have something to lose. You are already naked. There is no reason not to follow your heart.

I dedicate this work to the Prophet Muhammad (Peace Be Upon Him), Mercy to all the Creation, who has been the source of inspiration and guidance to humanity.

May the Knowledge delivered by me shall be a continuing blessing for me in the Life Hereafter (Ameen).

With Love and Care,

Muhammad Zain

SECTION A – FOUNDATIONS OF INTERNAL AUDITING (WEIGHTAGE 15%)

STUDY POINTS

S.No	Study Questions	Study Answers
1.	What is the full form of **IPPF**?	The full form of IPPF is International Professional Practices Framework.
2.	Define **IPPF**?	IPPF is the conceptual framework that organizes the authoritative guidance promulgated by The IIA. Authoritative Guidance comprises of two categories mandatory guidance and recommended guidance.
3.	What is **Mandatory guidance**?	Conformance with the principles outlined in mandatory guidance is required and essential for the professional practice of internal auditing. Mandatory guidance is developed following an established due diligence process, which includes a period of public exposure for stakeholder input.
4.	What are the elements of **Mandatory Guidance**?	There are four elements of Mandatory guidance: 1. Core Principles for the Professional Practice of Internal Auditing 2. Definition of Internal Auditing 3. Code of Ethics 4. International Standards for the Professional Practice of Internal Auditing (Standards).

5.	What is **recommended guidance**?	Recommended guidance describes practices for implementing the IIA's Core Principles, Definition of Internal Auditing, Code of Ethics, and *Standards*.
6.	What are the **recommended elements** of IPPF?	The recommended elements of the IPPF are: • Implementation Guidance — assist internal auditors in applying the *Standards*. • Supplemental Guidance (Practice Guides) — provide detailed processes and procedures for internal audit practitioners.
7.	What is the **Mission** of Internal Audit?	To *enhance and protect organizational value by providing risk-based and objective assurance, advice, and insight.* The Mission of Internal Audit articulates what internal audit aspires to accomplish within an organization. Its place in the New IPPF is deliberate, demonstrating how practitioners should leverage the entire framework to facilitate their ability to achieve the Mission.
8.	What is the **definition** of Internal Auditing?	Internal auditing is an independent, objective assurance and consulting activity designed to add value and improve an organization's operations. It helps an organization accomplish its objectives by bringing a systematic, disciplined approach to evaluate and improve the effectiveness of risk management, control, and governance processes. The Definition of Internal Auditing states the fundamental purpose, nature, and scope of internal auditing.

9.	What are the **Standards**?	The **Standards** are principle-focused and provide a framework for performing and promoting internal auditing. The *Standards* are mandatory requirements consisting of: • Statements of basic requirements for the professional practice of internal auditing and evaluating the effectiveness of its performance. The requirements are internationally applicable to organizations and individuals. • Interpretations, which clarify terms or concepts within the statements. • Glossary Terms.
10.	What are the **purposes** of the *Standards*?	The purposes of Standards are: 1. Guide adherence with the mandatory elements of the International Professional Practices Framework. 2. Provide a framework for performing and promoting a broad range of value-added internal auditing services. 3. Establish the basis for the evaluation of internal audit performance. 4. Foster improved organizational processes and operations.
11.	What do the **Standards** consist of?	Standards consist of the following items: **1. Statements** of core requirements for the professional practice of internal auditing and for evaluating the effectiveness of performance that are internationally

		applicable at organizational and individual levels. 2. **Interpretations** are clarifying terms or concepts within the *Standards*.
12.	What are the three **types** of *Standards*?	The three types of Standards are: 1. Attribute Standards 2. Performance Standards 3. Implementation Standards
13.	At what **level**, Standards are applicable?	The *Standards* apply to individual internal auditors and the internal audit activity. All internal auditors are accountable for conforming with the standards related to individual objectivity, proficiency, and due professional care and the standards relevant to the performance of their job responsibilities. Chief audit executives are additionally accountable for the internal audit activity's overall conformance with the *Standards*.
14.	Define the **Attribute standards**?	**Attribute Standards** address the attributes of organizations and individuals performing internal auditing.
15.	Define the **Performance standards**?	**Performance Standards** describe the nature of internal auditing and provide quality criteria against which the performance of these services can be measured.
16.	Define the **Implementation standards**?	**Implementation Standards** expand upon the Attribute and Performance Standards by providing the requirements applicable to assurance or consulting services.

17.	What are the primary components of **Attribute Standards**?	The **primary components** of the Attribute Standards are: • **Purpose, Authority, and Responsibility (1000).** The purpose, authority, and responsibility of the IAA should be formally defined in the internal audit charter, consistent with the *Standards*, and approved by the board. • **Independence and Objectivity (1100).** The IAA must be independent, and the internal auditors must be objective in performing their work. • **Proficiency and Due Professional Care (1200).** The engagement must be performed with proficiency and due professional care. • **Quality Assurance and Improvement Program (1300).** The Chief Audit Executive (CAE, the head of the IAA) must develop and maintain a quality assurance and improvement program that covers all aspects of the internal audit activity and continuously monitors its effectiveness.
18.	What are the primary components of **Performance Standards**?	The **primary components** of the Performance Standards are: • **Managing the Internal Audit Activity (2000).** The CAE must effectively manage the internal audit activity to ensure that it adds value to the organization. • **Nature of Work (2100).** The internal audit activity must evaluate and contribute to improving risk management, control, and governance processes using a systematic and disciplined approach.

		• **Engagement Planning (2200).** Internal auditors must develop and record a plan for each engagement, including the scope, objectives, timing, and resource allocations. • **Performing the Engagement (2300).** Internal auditors must identify, analyze, evaluate, and record sufficient information to achieve the engagement's objectives. • **Communicating Results (2400).** Internal auditors must communicate the engagement results. • **Monitoring Progress (2500).** The CAE must establish and maintain a system to monitor the disposition of results communicated to management. • **Resolution of Management's Acceptance of Risks (2600).** When the CAE believes that senior management has accepted a level of residual risk that may be unacceptable to the organization, the CAE must discuss the matter with senior management. If the decision regarding residual risk is not resolved, the CAE and senior management must report the matter to the board for resolution.
19.	What are the ten **core principles** that guide the Internal Audit Activity (IAA)?	The ten core principles are: 1. Demonstrates integrity. 2. Demonstrates competence and due professional care. 3. Is objective and free from undue influence (independent).

		4. Aligns with the strategies, objectives, and risks of the organization.
		5. Is appropriately positioned and adequately resourced.
		6. Demonstrates quality and continuous improvement.
		7. Communicates effectively.
		8. Provides risk-based assurance.
		9. Is insightful, proactive, and future-focused.
		10. Promotes organizational development.
20.	What are the two types of **Recommended Guidance**?	The two types of Recommended Guidance are: 1. Implementation Guidance 2. Supplemental Guidance
21.	What is the **Implementation Guidance**?	Implementation Guidance assists internal auditors in applying the *Standards*. Implementation Guidance collectively addresses internal auditing's approach, methodologies, and consideration but does not detail processes or procedures.
22.	What is **Supplemental Guidance**?	Supplemental Guidance provides detailed guidance for conducting internal audit activities. These include topical areas, sector-specific issues, processes and procedures, tools and techniques, programs, step-by-step approaches, and examples of deliverables.

23.	What is the **purpose, authority, and responsibility** of Internal Audit Activity?	The purpose, authority, and responsibility of the internal audit activity must be formally defined in an internal audit charter, consistent with the Mission of Internal Audit and the mandatory elements of the International Professional Practices Framework (the Core Principles for the Professional Practice of Internal Auditing, the Code of Ethics, the Standards, and the Definition of Internal Auditing). The chief audit executive must periodically review the internal audit charter and present it to senior management and the board for approval.
24.	What is an **Internal Audit charter**?	The internal audit charter is a formal document that defines the internal audit activity's purpose, authority, and responsibility. The internal audit charter establishes the internal audit activity's position within the organization, including the nature of the chief audit executive's functional reporting relationship with the board; authorizes access to records, personnel, and physical properties relevant to the performance of engagements; and defines the scope of internal audit activities. Final approval of the internal audit charter resides with the board.
25.	Who **writes** the Internal Audit Charter, and who **approves** it?	The charter should be written by (and periodically reviewed by) the CAE and approved by senior management and the board or audit committee.
26.	What are the **seven sections** in the Internal Audit Charter?	The seven sections in Internal Audit Charter are: **1. Purpose and Mission** – it includes the mission of internal auditing and the definition of internal auditing

		2. Standards for the Professional Practice of Internal Auditing – establishes that the internal audit activity will follow all the mandatory elements of IPPF. Furthermore, the Chief Audit Executive must report periodically to the board about the internal audit activity's conformance with the Standards and Code of Ethics. **3. Authority** – establishes the dual reporting responsibility of internal audit activity. **4. Independence and Objectivity** – The internal audit activity must have organizational independence, and internal auditors maintain objectivity. **5. Scope of Internal Audit Activities** – includes the provision of assurance and consulting engagements. **6. Responsibility** – highlights the specific responsibilities of the Chief Audit Executive. **7. Quality Assurance and Improvement Program** – ensures that the internal auditors perform engagements at an accepted level of quality and excellence.
27.	What are the **characteristics** of Internal Audit Charter?	The Charter should: • Establish the internal audit activity's position within the organization, including the nature of the CAE's functional reporting relationship with the board. • Authorize access to records, personnel, and physical properties relevant to the performance of engagements.

		• Define the scope of internal audit activities.
28.	How is **conformance** with the Charter and Mandatory Guidance demonstrated?	Conformance with the charter and the Mandatory Guidance may be demonstrated through the minutes of meetings with senior management and the board.
29.	What is the definition of **Assurance Services**?	"An objective examination of evidence to provide an independent assessment on governance, risk management, and control processes for the organization.
30.	What are the **examples** of Assurance Engagements?	Some of the examples of Assurance Engagements are: • Risk and control assessments • Audits of third parties and contract compliance • Security and privacy audits • Performance and quality audits • Key performance indicator audits • Operational audits • Financial audits • Regulatory compliance audits
31.	How many **parties** are involved in **Assurance Services**?	Three parties are involved in assurance services: 1. the person or group directly involved with the entity, operation, function, process, system, or other subject matter—**the process owner**; 2. the person or group making the assessment—**the internal auditor**; and 3. the person or group using the assessment—

		the user.
32.	What is the definition of **Consulting Services**?	"Advisory and related client services, the nature and scope of which are agreed upon with the client and which are intended to add value and improve an organization's operations. In a **consulting engagement**, the auditor provides advice or makes a suggestion. **The auditor does not need to be independent in a consulting engagement.** **Consulting services do not impair the objectivity of either the internal auditor or the IAA.** Furthermore, consultancy services can only be provided if it is **specifically defined** in the Internal Audit Charter.
33.	What are the examples of **Consulting Engagements**?	Some of the examples of Consulting Engagements are: • Training • System design • System development • Due diligence • Privacy • Benchmarking • Internal control assessments • Process mapping
34.	How many **parties** are involved in **Consultancy Services**?	Consulting services generally involve two parties: 1. the person or group offering the advice—**the internal auditor**; and

		2. the person or group seeking and receiving the advice—**the engagement client**.
35.	What is the **difference between** Assurance and Consulting engagements?	In an **assurance engagement**, the auditor provides an assessment and states an opinion about whether or not something within the company is operating or performing correctly. The auditor should be objective in the investigation and independent in the decision.

In a **consulting engagement**, the auditor provides advice or makes a suggestion. |
| 36. | What is the **Code of Ethics**? | "The Code of Ethics states the principles and expectations governing the behaviour of individuals and organizations in the conduct of internal auditing. It describes the minimum requirements for conduct and behavioural expectations rather than specific activities." |
| 37. | What are the **four principles** in the Code of Ethics? | The four principles in the Code of Ethics are:

1. Integrity
2. Objectivity
3. Confidentiality
4. Competency |
| 38. | What are the rules of conduct related to **Integrity**? | Internal auditors:

• Shall perform their work with honesty, diligence, and responsibility.

• Shall observe the law and make disclosures expected by the law and the profession.

• Shall not knowingly be a party to any illegal activity or engage in acts that are discreditable to the profession of internal auditing or to the organization. |

		• Shall respect and contribute to the legitimate and ethical objectives of the organization.
39.	What are the rules of conduct related to **Objectivity**?	Internal auditors: • Shall not participate in any activity or relationship that may impair or be presumed to impair their unbiased assessment. This participation includes those activities or relationships that may conflict with the interests of the organization. • Shall not accept anything that may impair or be presumed to impair their professional judgment. • Shall disclose all material facts known to them that, if not disclosed, may distort the reporting of activities under review. The internal auditor should maintain objectivity and not assume management responsibility when performing **Consulting Services**.
40.	What are the rules of conduct related to **Confidentiality**?	Internal auditors: • Shall be prudent in the use and protection of information acquired in the course of their duties. • Shall not use the information for any personal gain or in any manner that would be contrary to the law or detrimental to the legitimate and ethical objectives of the organization.

41.	What are the rules of conduct related to **Competency**?	Internal auditors: • Shall engage only in those services for which they have the necessary knowledge, skills, and experience. • Shall perform internal auditing services following the International Standards for the Professional Practice of Internal Auditing. • Shall continually improve their proficiency and the effectiveness and quality of their services.
42.	What are the **considerations** for the implementation of **rules of conduct** for the CAE in case of **integrity**?	The considerations for CAE in the case of integrity are: • The CAE must ensure that the internal audit activity achieves its purpose, fulfills the responsibilities included in the internal audit charter and that its members conform with the Code of Ethics and the *Standards*. • The CAE should cultivate a culture of integrity by acting with integrity and adhering to the Code of Ethics. • The CAE may bring about awareness and accountability by requiring internal auditors to acknowledge in writing that they have reviewed and understood the policies and procedures of the IAA. If this is implemented, the IAA can show diligence and responsibility. • The CAE may require internal auditors to acknowledge in writing their agreement to follow The IIA's Code of Ethics and any additional ethics-related policies specific to the IAA.

		• The CAE may emphasize the importance of integrity by providing training that demonstrates integrity and other ethical principles in action. • The CAE should maintain a working environment where internal auditors feel supported when expressing legitimate, evidence-based observations, conclusions, and opinions, even if they are not favourable.
43.	What are the **considerations** for implementing **rules of conduct** for the CAE in the case of **Objectivity**?	The considerations for CAE in case of objectivity are: • The CAE may create relevant policies and procedures, such as internal auditors receiving gifts, favours, and rewards. • The CAE may require internal auditors to complete an acknowledgement form disclosing potential conflicts of interest and impairments to objectivity, and the CAE should consider these disclosures when assigning internal auditors to engagements. • The CAE should carefully consider how performance measures and the system of compensation may influence internal auditors' objectivity when developing policies and procedures. • The CAE enforces objectivity and requires that potential impairments be declared, even If the work is outsourced or co-sourced. The CAE may include such requirements in third-party provider contracts and should research the providers' relationship to determine whether conflicts of interest exist.

44.	What are the **considerations** for the implementation of **rules of conduct** for the CAE in case of **Confidentiality**?	The considerations for CAE in case of confidentiality are: • The CAE should consult with legal counsel to better understand the impact of legal and regulatory requirements and protections of information. The organization's policies and procedures may require that specific positions in the company review and approve business information before the external release of that information. • The CAE may implement additional policies, processes, and procedures that the internal audit activity and external consultants must follow. Typically, these are closely aligned with the Mandatory Guidance. • The CAE should periodically assess and confirm internal auditors' need for access to areas and databanks containing confidential information. The CAE should confirm that access controls are working effectively. • The CAE is to control access to the engagement records, in part by developing requirements for retaining the records, regardless of the medium in which each record is stored. • The CAE and internal auditors need to be able to comply with requests by regulators and with transparency laws in public sector organizations. • The CAE may discuss the principles, rules, policies, and expectations related to confidentiality during meetings or trainings of the IAA also may use the opportunity to brainstorm and discuss the potential impact

		of sharing various types of confidential organizational information. • The CAE may require internal auditors to sign a form acknowledging that they attended such sessions and understand relevant policies, procedures, and expectations.
45.	What are the **considerations** for implementing **rules of conduct** for the CAE in the case of **Competency**?	The considerations for CAE in case of competency are: • The CAE is responsible for ensuring the competency of the internal audit activity as a whole. • The CAE should develop a staffing strategy to regularly assess the competencies of individual internal auditors, the internal audit activity as a whole, and any service providers upon which the internal audit activity relies. • The CAE should inventory the skills and experience of individual auditors, align them with the competencies needed to fulfill the internal audit plan, and identify any gaps in coverage. • The CAE may address deficiencies by providing training and mentorship, rotating internal audit staff, bringing in guest auditors, and hiring external service providers. Also, the CAE should encourage education and training opportunities when possible. • The CAE should develop policies and procedures that regularly review individual performance, involving benchmarking and reviewing key performance indicators.

		• The CAE should implement a quality assurance and improvement program to promote the continual improvement of the internal audit activity. The CAE may use The IIA's Competency Framework to benchmark the maturity of the IAA and work toward its progress.
46.	What are the **considerations** for implementing **rules of conduct** for the Individual Internal Auditors in the case of **Integrity**?	• For internal auditors, integrity may be primarily a personal attribute, making it difficult to measure, enforce, or guarantee. • For individual internal auditors, the best attempts to identify and measure integrity likely involve astute awareness and understanding of the Code of Ethics' rules of conduct for integrity, the Mandatory Guidance, and supporting practices. • For internal auditors, some behaviours may not be illegal but may be discreditable. • Internal auditors should adhere to the ethics policy, code of conduct, values statement, and other policies and procedures established by the IAA and the organization (i.e., human resources and legal policies). • Internal auditors must abide by the laws and regulations relevant to the industry and jurisdictions within which the organization operates. • Internal auditors should consider how strategies and objectives align with the organization's mission and values and should identify opportunities to make significant improvements to its governance, risk management, and control processes.

Muhammad Zain

		• Internal auditors may support their understanding of the Code of Ethics and their ability to conform with its tenets by participating in ethics-focused continuing professional education/development (CPE/CPD).
47.	What are the **considerations** for implementing **rules of conduct** for the Individual Internal Auditors in case of **Objectivity**?	• Internal auditors are to perform engagements in a manner that results in a balanced assessment of all the relevant circumstances, and the engagement work papers that have been approved by the CAE or a designated engagement supervisor should evidence that balanced assessment. • Internal auditors are to review relevant resources as this may help to recognize better, understand, and overcome innate biases and subjectivity. • Internal auditors should not be unduly influenced by others or subordinate their judgment on audit matters to others. • Internal auditors should avoid conflicts of interest, including excessive individual fraternizing outside of work with the organization's employees, management, third-party suppliers, and vendors. Close relationships or financial ties, such as investments, could represent conflicts of interest, whether in fact or perception. If unavoidable, such objectivity impairments should be disclosed. • Internal auditors shall not accept anything that may impair or be presumed to impair their professional judgment. Examples include accepting gifts, meals, trips, and

		special treatment that exceed policy limits or are not disclosed and approved. • Internal auditors are to disclose any "material" facts about the activities under review. Internal auditors must not hold back from reporting all the known facts pertinent to the engagement results and conclusions, even if those facts, results, or conclusions may be displeasing to senior management and the board. • Internal audit communications should be clear, factual, and objective, avoiding language that could minimize, hide, or exaggerate findings.
48.	What are the **considerations** for implementing **rules of conduct** for the Individual Internal Auditors in case of **Confidentiality**?	• Internal auditors should understand the laws and regulations related to confidentiality and information security for the jurisdictions in which their organization operates, as well as know any policies specific to their organization and internal audit activity. Such policies may identify, for example, the type of information that may be disclosed, the parties that must authorize the disclosure, and the procedures to be followed. • Internal auditors should follow the policies and procedures set by the organization and the CAE, as well as comply with any relevant laws and regulations. • Internal auditors collect only the data required to perform the assigned engagement and use this information only for the engagement's intended purposes. • Internal auditors protect information from intentional or unintentional disclosure

through the use of controls such as data encryption, email distribution restrictions, and restriction of physical access to the information.

• Internal auditors eliminate copies of or access to data when it is no longer needed.

• Internal auditors should consider confidentiality when documenting internal audit work and observations. Work program or engagement work paper templates may include reminders about confidentiality; electronic formats may contain automated controls that require internal auditors to acknowledge such reminders before auditors can access and complete documentation.

• Internal auditors are required to establish a written understanding of the restrictions related to the distribution of engagement results and the access to engagement records, specifically when they are planning an assurance engagement that involves third parties, as they might need to release the results of an assurance engagement to parties outside the organization.

• Internal auditors must stipulate limitations regarding how the results may be distributed and used. They must follow established procedures for disclosure, including contacting the proper authority in the organization for written permission before disclosing any information and retaining the authorization in work papers.

• Internal auditors must not use any information for personal gain.

| 49. | What are the **considerations** for implementing **rules of conduct** for the Individual Internal Auditors in case of **Competency**? | • Internal auditors should regularly assess themselves to gain insight into their level of competency, proficiency, and effectiveness and to find areas for potential growth. The IIA's Competency Framework may be a useful benchmarking tool for this purpose.

• Internal auditors should seek constructive formal/informal feedback from peers, supervisors, and the CAE. Feedback may be given throughout engagements, during supervisory reviews, and after closing engagements.

• Internal auditors assigned to plan an engagement must determine the competencies needed to achieve the engagement objectives. In engagement work papers, internal auditors conducting an engagement may document their rationale for the resource allocation used.

• When resources appear to be insufficient, internal auditors should consult with the CAE and document the discussion results. If appropriate and sufficient resources are not available, it may be necessary to seek additional resources outside the internal audit activity.

• Internal auditors may build their competencies by pursuing education, mentorship, and supervised work experiences. Correctly supervised internal audit engagements play a significant role in facilitating the development of internal auditors because most internal audit activities have limited resources. |

		• Internal auditors are responsible for taking the necessary actions to obtain any continuing professional education and development (CPE/CPD) hours they may need. • Internal auditors are responsible for their conformance with the Code of Ethics and relevant standards and for obtaining the knowledge, skills, and experience needed to perform their responsibilities and to improve their proficiency and quality of service continually. • Internal auditors may create and maintain plans for their professional development.

SECTION A – FOUNDATIONS OF INTERNAL AUDITING (WEIGHTAGE 15%)

TRUE / FALSE QUESTIONS AND ANSWERS

S.No	Questions	Answers
1.	Conformance with the principles outlined in mandatory guidance is required but not essential for the professional practice of internal auditing.	**FALSE.** Conformance with the principles outlined in mandatory guidance is required and **essential** for the professional practice of internal auditing.
2.	There are four elements of mandatory guidance.	**TRUE.** There are four elements of **Mandatory guidance**: 1. Core Principles for the Professional Practice of Internal Auditing 2. Definition of Internal Auditing 3. Code of Ethics 4. International Standards for the Professional Practice of Internal Auditing (Standards).
3.	The mission of Internal Audit is to enhance and protect organizational value by providing risk-based and	**FALSE.** The mission of Internal Audit is *To enhance and protect organizational value by providing risk-based and **objective** assurance, advice, and insight.*

ZAIN ACADEMY
Knowledge For All

	absolute assurance, advice, and insight.	
4.	The complete form of IPPF is International Professional Practices Framework.	**TRUE.** IPPF stands for International Professional Practices Framework.
5.	The *Standards* are rule-focused and provide a framework for performing and promoting internal auditing.	**FALSE.** The *Standards* are **principle**-focused and provide a framework for performing and promoting internal auditing.
6.	There are three types of Standards.	**TRUE. Attribute**, **Performance**, and **Implementation** Standards.
7.	The standards apply to Internal Audit activity.	**FALSE.** The *Standards* apply to individual **internal auditors** and the **internal audit activity**.
8.	Ten core principles guide the Internal Audit Activity (IAA).	**TRUE.** Ten core principles guide the Internal Audit Activity (IAA).
9.	There are three types of recommended guidance.	**FALSE.** There are **two** types of recommended guidance, i.e. Implemental and Supplemental guidance.
10.	Implementation Guides details the policies and procedures.	**FALSE.** Implementation Guides assist internal auditors in **applying** the *Standards*. IGs collectively address internal auditing's approach, methodologies, and consideration but **do not** detail processes or procedures.

11.	Supplemental Guidance provides limited guidance for conducting internal audit activities.	**FALSE.** Supplemental Guidance provides **detailed** guidance for conducting internal audit activities.
12.	Internal auditing is an independent, reasonable assurance and consulting activity designed to add value and improve an organization's operations.	**FALSE.** Internal auditing is an **independent, objective assurance** and **consulting activity** designed to add value and improve an organization's operations.
13.	The Definition of Internal Auditing states the fundamental purpose, nature, and scope of internal auditing.	**TRUE.** The Definition of Internal Auditing states the fundamental **purpose**, **nature**, and **scope** of internal auditing.
14.	Audit Committee writes the Internal Audit Charter.	**FALSE.** The charter should be **written** by (and periodically reviewed by) the **CAE** and **approved** by **senior management** and the **board** or audit committee.
15.	There are eight sections in Internal Audit Charter?	**FALSE.** There are **seven sections** in Internal Audit Charter. 1. Purpose and Mission 2. Standards for the Professional Practice of Internal Auditing 3. Authority

		4. Independence and Objectivity 5. Scope of Internal Audit Activities 6. Responsibility 7. Quality Assurance and Improvement Program.
16.	Assurance services are a subjective examination of the evidence to provide an independent assessment on governance, risk management, and control processes for the organization.	**FALSE.** Assurance services is an **objective examination** of the evidence to provide an independent assessment on governance, risk management, and control processes for the organization.
17.	There are three parties involved in Assurance Services.	**TRUE.** There are **three parties** involved in assurance services, i.e. process owner, internal auditor, and user.
18.	Consulting Services expresses an opinion on the matter being tested.	**FALSE.** Consulting services provides **advice** or makes a **suggestion**.
19.	The auditor needs to be independent in consulting engagement.	**FALSE.** The auditor **does not** need to be independent in a consulting engagement.
20.	Consulting services do not impair the objectivity of	**TRUE.** Consulting services **do not** impair the objectivity of either the internal auditor or the IAA.

	either the internal auditor or the IAA.	
21.	Consulting services can be performed even if not defined in Internal Audit Charter.	**FALSE.** The Standards state that internal auditors can **only** perform consulting services specifically defined in the internal audit charter.
22.	The Code of Ethics states the principles and suggestions governing the behaviour of individuals and organizations in the conduct of internal auditing.	**FALSE.** "The Code of Ethics states the principles and **expectations** governing the behaviour of individuals and organizations in the conduct of internal auditing. It describes the minimum requirements for conduct and behavioural expectations rather than specific activities."
23.	There are four principles in the Code of Ethics.	**TRUE.** The four principles are Integrity, Objectivity, Confidentiality and Competency.
24.	Internal Auditors may not knowingly be a party to any illegal activity or engage in acts that are discreditable to the profession of internal auditing or to the organization.	**FALSE.** Internal Auditors **shall not** knowingly be a party to any illegal activity or engage in acts that are discreditable to the profession of internal auditing or the organization.
25.	Internal Auditors shall not participate in any activity or	**TRUE.** Internal Auditors **shall not** participate in any activity or relationship that may impair or be presumed to impair their unbiased assessment. This participation includes those

	relationship that may impair or be presumed to impair their unbiased assessment.	activities or relationships that may conflict with the interests of the organization.
26.	Internal Auditors can use the information for any personal gain or in any manner that would be contrary to the law or detrimental to the legitimate and ethical objectives of the organization.	**FALSE.** Internal Auditors **shall not use** the information for any personal gain or in any manner that would be contrary to the law or detrimental to the legitimate and ethical objectives of the organization.
27.	Internal auditors can engage only in those services for which they have the necessary knowledge, skills, and experience.	**TRUE.** Internal auditors can engage only in those services for which they have the necessary **knowledge, skills, and experience.**
28.	The proper organizational role of internal auditing is to serve as the investigative arm of the board of directors.	**FALSE.** The primary role of the internal audit activity is to assist the management of a company in maintaining effective controls by evaluating the effectiveness of those controls. In this role, it serves as an **appraisal function** that adds **value** to operations.
29.	The external auditor benefits because the internal audit	**FALSE.** Internal auditors cannot **provide an opinion** about the accuracy and completeness of the annual financial

	activity can provide an opinion about the accuracy and completeness of the annual financial statements.	statement. This is solely the responsibility of the external auditor.
30.	Internal auditing activity gives management assurance that there is reasonable control over day-to-day operations.	**TRUE.** Internal audit activities can assist the management of a company to maintain effective controls by evaluating the effectiveness of those controls with the goal of **continuous improvement**.
31.	The authority of the internal audit activity is limited to that granted by the audit committee and the chief financial officer.	**FALSE.** Management and the board of directors grant authority to the internal audit activity through the **internal audit activity's charter**.
32.	An element of authority that should be included in the charter of the internal audit activity (IAA) is identifying the organizational units where engagements are to be performed.	**FALSE.** The charter should establish the internal audit activity's **position within the organization**; authorize access to records, personnel, and physical properties relevant to the performance of engagements, and define the scope of internal audit activities. Final approval of the internal audit charter resides with the board.
33.	The length of tenure of the chief audit executive is	**FALSE.** The charter defines the purpose, authority, and responsibility of the IAA (PA 1000-1). Specifying the length of tenure of the

	included in Internal Audit Charter.	CAE will **not be as important** as defining the IAA's purpose, authority and responsibility.
34.	A primary reason for establishing an internal audit activity (IAA) is to relieve overburdened management of the responsibility for establishing effective controls.	**FALSE. Evaluate and improve the effectiveness of control processes.** This is the primary reason for establishing the internal audit activity. The internal auditing activity "helps an organization accomplish its objectives by bringing a systematic, disciplined approach to evaluate and improve the effectiveness of risk management, control, and governance processes."
35.	Audit committees are most likely to participate in the approval of the appointment of the chief audit executive.	**TRUE.** The independence of the internal audit activity is enhanced when the audit committee **participates in naming the CAE.**
36.	The purposes of the *Standards* include guiding the ethical conduct of internal auditors.	**FALSE.** Guiding the ethical conduct of the internal auditors is **not one of the four purposes of the Standards.** The four purposes include: (1) Delineate basic principles that represent the practice of internal auditing as it should be; (2) Provide a framework for performing and promoting a broad range of value-added internal audit activities; (3) Establish the basis for the measurement of internal audit performance; and (4) Foster improved organizational processes and operations.
37.	The Rules of Conduct outlined in The IIA Code of	**FALSE.** The Rules of Conduct outlined in The IIA Code of Ethics describe the **behaviour norms** expected of internal auditors. These rules aid in interpreting the principles into

	Ethics are guidelines to assist internal auditors in dealing with engagement clients.	practical applications and are intended to guide the ethical conduct of the internal auditors.
38.	The length of tenure for the chief audit executive is specified in the internal audit charter.	**FALSE.** The charter **does not specify** the length of tenure of the chief audit executive.
39.	A written charter approved by the board that formally defines the internal audit activity's purpose, authority, and responsibility enhances its Independence.	**TRUE.** The internal audit charter establishes the **IAA's position within the organization**; authorizes access to records, personnel, and physical properties relevant to the performance of engagements, and defines the scope of internal audit activities.
40.	The Standards state that internal auditors should be involved with reviewing quarterly financial statements.	**FALSE.** The *Standards* **do not specifically** mention that internal auditors should be involved in reviewing the quarterly financial statements.
41.	Having a material ownership interest in a competitor is most likely a violation of The	**TRUE.** Having a material ownership interest in a competitor is most likely a **violation of the code of ethics** for an internal auditor. The material ownership position in a major competitor will impair the auditor's objectivity.

	IIA Code of Ethics.	
42.	Designing and implementing appropriate controls is a responsibility of the Internal Audit Activity.	**FALSE.** Designing and implementing appropriate controls is not an appropriate responsibility for the IIA. This is the **responsibility of management**.
43.	Protecting organizational value is a part of the Mission of Internal Audit.	**TRUE.** The Mission of Internal Audit is to **enhance and protect organizational value** by providing risk-based and objective assurance, advice, and insight.

SECTION B – INDEPENDENCE AND OBJECTIVITY (WEIGHTAGE 15%)

STUDY POINTS

S.No	Study Questions	Study Answers
1.	What is the requirement of Standard 1100 – **Independence and Objectivity**?	The internal audit activity must be independent, and internal auditors must be objective in performing their work.
2.	What is **Independence**?	"Independence is the freedom from conditions that threaten the ability of the internal audit activity to carry out internal audit responsibilities in an unbiased manner. To achieve the degree of independence necessary to carry out the responsibilities of the internal audit activity effectively, the chief audit executive has direct and unrestricted access to senior management and the board. This can be achieved through a dual-reporting relationship. Threats to independence must be managed at the individual auditor, engagement, functional, and organizational levels."
3.	What is **Objectivity**?	"Objectivity is an unbiased mental attitude that allows internal auditors to perform engagements in such a manner that they believe in their work product and that no quality compromises are made. Objectivity requires that internal auditors do not subordinate their judgment on audit matters to others. Threats to objectivity must be managed at the individual auditor, engagement, functional, and organizational levels."

4.	What does **Organizational Independence** mean?	Organizational Independence means that the internal audit activity must not have any current or previous relationships with the departments that it audits. Organizational independence can be achieved through a properly designed Internal Audit Charter.
5.	Who does the **CAE** report to?	The CAE should report to an **audit committee, or its equivalent, for any functional and engagement issues**. For **administrative** issues, the CAE should report to the CEO (or a similar position).
6.	What are **examples** of functional reporting?	The examples of Functional Reporting are: • Approving the internal audit charter; • Approving the risk-based internal audit plan; • Approving the internal audit budget and resource plan; • Receiving communications from the chief audit executive on the internal audit activity's performance relative to its plan and other matters; • Approving decisions regarding the appointment and removal of the chief audit executive; • Approving the remuneration of the chief audit executive; and

		• Making appropriate inquiries of management and the chief audit executive to determine the inappropriate scope or resource limitations.
7.	What are **examples** of administrative reporting?	The examples of Administrative Reporting are: • Budgeting and management accounting. • Human resource administration, including personnel evaluations and compensation. • Internal communications and information flows. • Administration of the internal audit activity's policies and procedures.
8.	What is the requirement of Standard 1110 – **Organizational Independence**?	**The chief audit executive must report to a level within the organization that allows the internal audit activity to fulfill its responsibilities.** The chief audit executive must confirm to the board, at least annually, the organizational independence of the internal audit activity. The internal audit activity must be free from interference in determining the scope of internal auditing, performing work, and communicating results. The chief audit executive must disclose such interference to the board and discuss the implications.
9.	What is **Individual Objectivity**?	"Internal auditors must have an impartial, unbiased attitude and avoid any conflict of interest."
10.	What are the requirements of standard 1130 –	If independence or objectivity is impaired in fact or appearance, the **impairment details must be disclosed to appropriate parties**. The

	Impairment to Independence or Objectivity?	nature of the disclosure will depend upon the impairment.
11.	What are **common impairments** to Independence and Objectivity?	The common impairments to Independence and Objectivity are: 1. A personal conflict of interest. 2. A scope limitation, including a restriction of access to records, personnel, or properties. 3. Resource limitation, which includes funding limitations. 4. Situations where the auditor is assessing operations for which they were previously responsible. 5. Assurance engagements for functions over which the CAE previously had responsibility. 6. Consulting engagements in areas where assurance engagements are also performed.
12.	What shall be the Internal Auditor's course of action if he believes that independence or objectivity has been **impaired**?	If an auditor believes that independence or objectivity has been impaired, the auditor must disclose the nature of the impairment to the CAE or appropriate parties. If an impairment arises during an engagement, it must be reported immediately to the engagement manager so that the situation can be addressed or eliminated.
13.	What is a **Conflict of Interest**?	A situation in which an internal auditor, who is in a position of trust, has a competing professional or personal interest. Such competing interests can make it challenging to fulfill their duties impartially. A conflict of interest exists even if no unethical or improper act results. A conflict of interest can

		create an appearance of impropriety that can undermine confidence in the internal auditor, the internal audit activity, and the profession. A conflict of interest could impair an individual's ability to perform their duties and responsibilities objectively.
14.	What is the auditor's **responsibility** if a conflict of interest arises in assurance and consulting engagements?	An auditor with a conflict of interest in an assurance engagement should be removed. The auditor can be reassigned back to the engagement if the conflict is resolved. Any conflicts of interest in a consulting engagement should be disclosed to the client. If the client has no objections, then the auditor may remain on the consulting engagement.
15.	What is **Scope Limitation**?	A **scope limitation** is a restriction on the engagement that prevents accomplishing the objectives and plans.
16.	What are the consequences of **resource limitations**?	Without sufficient resources and funding, the IAA may not be able to operate independently and objectively. For example, inadequate staffing, insufficient training, or outdated technology might invite compromises or shortcuts that would impair the IAA's position in the organization.
17.	May auditors **assess** operations that they were **previously responsible for**?	Internal auditors must refrain from assessing specific operations for which they were previously responsible. Objectivity is presumed to be impaired if an auditor provides assurance services for an activity for which the auditor had responsibility within the previous year. Objectivity is also impaired when auditors are auditing an area for which they will have

		future responsibility **within one year after** the engagement.
18.	May auditors provide **consulting** for operations that they were **previously responsible for**?	**Yes**, internal auditors may provide consulting services relating to operations for which they had previous responsibilities. If internal auditors have potential impairments to independence or objectivity relating to proposed consulting services, the disclosure must be made to the engagement client prior to accepting the engagement.
19.	Can internal auditors provide **assurance services** in areas of previously **consulting engagements**?	The internal audit activity may provide assurance services where it had previously performed consulting services, provided the nature of the consulting did not impair objectivity. It provided individual objectivity is managed when assigning resources to the engagement.
20.	What is the Chief Audit Executive's responsibility for **non-audit functions**?	It is possible that management could ask an internal auditor to assume responsibility for a part of operations that could be subject to periodic internal auditing assessments. Internal auditors **should not accept such assignments**, but management **may insist**. If the IAA accepts responsibility and the operation is part of the audit plan, the CAE could minimize the impairment to objectivity by using a third party to complete the audit (for example, an external auditor or third-party contractor). Also, the CAE should confirm that the individuals who have operational responsibility will not participate in any internal audits of the operation.

21.	What must be done if **Independence is impaired** in fact or in appearance?	"The details of the impairment must be disclosed to appropriate parties."
22.	What **responsibilities** does the CAE have to report Independence and Objectivity issues to the board?	The responsibilities of CAE are: 1. The CAE will confirm at least annually to the board that the IAA is organizationally independent. The CAE will need to make sure that the IAA maintains its organizational independence at all times. 2. The CAE will disclose to the board any interference with the IAA determining the scope of work, performing the work, or communicating the results.
23.	What is the requirement of Standard 1120 – **Individual Objectivity**?	Internal auditors must have an impartial, unbiased attitude and avoid any conflict of interest.
24.	Explain with examples how objectivity is impaired?	Examples of Objectivity impairment are as follows: • An internal auditor audits an area in which they recently worked, such as when an employee transfers into an internal audit from a different functional area of the organization and then is assigned to an audit of that function. • An internal auditor audits an area where a relative or close friend is employed. • An internal auditor assumes, without evidence, that an area being audited has effectively mitigated risks based solely on a

		prior positive audit or personal experiences (e.g., a lack of professional skepticism). • An internal auditor modifies the planned approach or results based on the undue influence of another person, often someone senior to the internal auditor, without appropriate justification.
25.	How can the Chief Audit Executive promote Objectivity in the Internal Audit department?	There are several ways that the CAE can promote and maintain objectivity within the IAA: • Job assignments should minimize potential conflicts of interest. For example, an auditor should not audit an area where their spouse works. • Information about potential conflicts of interest can be collected periodically. • Jobs should be rotated so that relationships do not develop between the auditor and the auditee that might impair the auditor's judgment. • A strong QAIP will help ensure that organizational independence and objectivity are part of the culture of the IAA.

SECTION B – INDEPENDENCE AND OBJECTIVITY (WEIGHTAGE 15%)

TRUE / FALSE QUESTIONS AND ANSWERS

S.No	Questions	Answers
1.	The internal audit activity must be independent, and internal auditors may be objective in performing their work.	**FALSE.** The internal audit activity must be independent, and internal auditors **must be** objective in performing their work.
2.	Independence is the freedom from conditions that limits the ability of the internal audit activity to carry out internal audit responsibilities in an unbiased manner.	**FALSE.** Independence is the freedom from conditions that **threaten** the ability of the internal audit activity to carry out internal audit responsibilities in an unbiased manner.
3.	The chief audit executive has direct and limited access to senior management and the board.	**FALSE.** The chief audit executive has direct and **unrestricted** access to senior management and the board.
4.	Objectivity is an unbiased mental attitude that allows internal auditors to perform engagements to believe in their work product and that no quality	**TRUE.** Objectivity is an **unbiased mental attitude** that allows internal auditors to perform engagements to believe in their work product and that no quality compromises are made.

	compromises are made.	
5.	Organizational Independence means that the internal audit activity may not have any current or previous relationships with the departments that it audits.	**FALSE.** Organizational Independence means that the internal audit activity **must not** have any current or previous relationships with the departments that it audits. Organizational independence can be achieved through a properly designed Internal Audit Charter.
6.	The CAE reports functionally to the CEO and administratively to the BOD.	**FALSE.** The CAE should report to an **audit committee, or its equivalent, for any functional and engagement issues.** For **administrative** issues, the CAE should report to the CEO (or a similar position).
7.	Internal auditors must have an impartial, unbiased attitude and avoid any conflict of interest.	**TRUE.** Internal auditors must have an **impartial, unbiased attitude** and avoid any **conflict of interest**.
8.	Objectivity is presumed to be impaired if an auditor provides assurance services for an activity for which the auditor had responsibility within the previous half-year.	**FALSE.** Objectivity is presumed to be impaired if an auditor provides assurance services for an activity for which the auditor had responsibility within the **previous year**.
9.	Objectivity is also impaired when auditors are	**TRUE.** Objectivity is also impaired when auditors are auditing an area for which they

	auditing an area for which they will have future responsibility **within one year after** the engagement.	will have future responsibility **within one year after** the engagement.
10.	Internal auditors may provide consulting services relating to operations for which they had previous responsibilities.	**TRUE.** Internal auditors may provide **consulting services** relating to operations for which they had **previous responsibilities**.
11.	The details of the impairment of Independence may not be disclosed to appropriate parties.	**FALSE.** The details of the impairment of Independence **must be** disclosed to appropriate parties.
12.	The CAE will confirm at least semi-annually to the board that the IAA is organizationally independent.	**FALSE.** The CAE will confirm **at least annually** to the board that the IAA is organizationally independent. The CAE will need to make sure that the IAA maintains its organizational independence at all times.
13.	An appropriate internal auditing role in a feasibility study is to participate in the drafting of recommendations for the computer acquisition and implementation.	**FALSE.** Internal auditors must consider standards of control and review procedures before implementation. But objectivity would be considered impaired if they would **design, install, draft procedures, or operate systems**. Therefore, ascertaining if the feasibility study addresses cost-benefit relationships would be an appropriate role for the internal auditor.
14.	The independence of	**FALSE.** Organizational status and objectivity permit members of the IAA to render the

Muhammad Zain

	the internal auditing activity is achieved through continuing professional development and due professional care.	**impartial** and **unbiased** judgments essential to the proper conduct of audits.
15.	An internal auditor's involvement in reengineering should include directing the implementation of the redesigned process.	**FALSE.** Internal auditors should not become **directly involved** in the **implementation** of the redesigned process. This would impair their independence and objectivity.
16.	An activity appropriately performed by the internal audit activity is reviewing systems of control before implementation.	**TRUE. Recommending standards of control** and **reviewing procedures** before implementation is not presumed to impair objectivity. However, an internal auditor's objectivity is presumed to be impaired by designing, installing, operating or drafting procedures for systems.

SECTION C – PROFICIENCY AND DUE PROFESSIONAL CARE (WEIGHTAGE 18%)

STUDY POINTS

S.No	Study Questions	Study Answers
1.	What are the requirements of Standard 1200 – **Proficiency and Due Professional Care**?	Engagements must be performed with proficiency and due professional care.
2.	What does Standard 1210 – **Proficiency** say about?	Internal auditors must possess the knowledge, skills, and other competencies needed to perform their individual responsibilities. The internal audit collectively must possess or obtain the knowledge, skills, and other competencies needed to perform its responsibilities.
3.	**Explain** the term Proficiency?	Proficiency is a collective term that refers to the knowledge, skills, and other competencies required of internal auditors to effectively carry out their professional responsibilities. It encompasses considering current activities, trends, and emerging issues, to enable relevant advice and recommendations. Internal auditors are encouraged to demonstrate their proficiency by obtaining appropriate professional certifications and qualifications, such as the Certified Internal Auditor designation and other designations offered by The Institute of Internal Auditors and other appropriate professional organizations.

4.	What is the internal auditor's responsibility relating to Proficiency in **assurance engagements**?	**The chief audit executive must obtain competent advice and assistance if the internal auditors lack the knowledge, skills, or other competencies needed to perform all or part of the engagement.** Internal auditors must have **sufficient knowledge to evaluate the risk of fraud** and how the organization manages it but is not expected to have the expertise of a person whose primary responsibility is detecting and investigating fraud. Internal auditors must have **sufficient knowledge of key information technology risks and controls** and available technology-based audit techniques to perform their assigned work. However, not all internal auditors are expected to have the expertise of an internal auditor whose primary responsibility is information technology auditing.
5.	What is the internal auditor's responsibility relating to Proficiency in **consulting engagements**?	The chief audit executive must decline the consulting engagement or obtain competent advice and assistance if the internal auditors lack the knowledge, skills, or other competencies needed to perform all or part of the engagement.
6.	What are the 10 **Competencies** in the Competency Framework?	1. Professional ethics – promotes and applies professional ethics. 2. Internal audit management – develops and manages the internal audit function. 3. IPPF – applies the IPPF framework.

		4. Governance, risk, and control – apply a thorough understanding of governance, risk and control appropriate to the organization.
		5. Business acumen – maintains expertise of the business environment, industry practices, and specific organizational factors.
		6. Communication – communicates with impact.
		7. Persuasion and collaboration – persuades and motivates others through collaboration and cooperation.
		8. Critical thinking – applies process analysis, business intelligence, and problem-solving techniques.
		9. Internal audit delivery – delivers internal audit engagements
		10. Improvement and innovation – embrace change and drive improvement and innovation.
7.	What are the three **levels of competence**?	The three levels of competence are: • **Proficiency**: The ability to apply knowledge to situations likely to be encountered and deal with them appropriately without extensive recourse to technical research and assistance. • **Understanding**: The ability to apply broad knowledge to situations likely to be encountered, recognize significant deviations, and carry out the research necessary to arrive at reasonable solutions.

		• **Appreciation**: The ability to recognize the existence of problems or potential problems and identify the additional research or assistance needed.
8.	What areas should an internal auditor have **proficiency** in?	Proficiency in applying: • Internal audit standards, • Procedures, and • Techniques in performing engagements.
9.	What should an internal auditor have an **understanding** of?	Management principles to **recognize and evaluate** the: • Materiality, and • Significance of deviations from good business practices.
10.	What areas should an internal auditor have an **appreciation** of?	• Accounting • Economics • Commercial law • Taxation • Finance • Quantitative methods • Information technology • Risk management • Fraud
11.	What **specific knowledge** should an internal auditor have?	Auditors must have knowledge: • To identify the indicators of fraud, and • Of crucial information technology risks and controls and available technology-based audit techniques.
12.	What **specific skills** should an	Internal Auditors shall have the following specific skills: • Dealing with people.

	internal auditor have?	• Understanding human relations. • Maintaining satisfactory relationships with engagement clients. • Communicating (both in oral and written form) to clearly and effectively convey engagement objectives, evaluations, conclusions, and recommendations.
13.	Who is responsible for **Proficiency and Due Professional Care** of the auditors?	The CAE is responsible for ensuring that each internal auditor and the IAA collectively have the necessary proficiencies to perform the engagements. The CAE determines the appropriate levels of education and experience required for an internal audit position. The CAE must also have confidence that the IAA staff collectively possesses the knowledge and skills necessary to perform their duties. If the CAE determines that the needed skills and competencies do not exist within the IAA, they must go outside the IAA to get them.
14.	When can the CAE **engage** external specialists?	If the IAA does not have the skills and competencies for an engagement, the CAE must either decline the engagement or go outside the IAA or organization to get those skills.
15.	What **must be considered** and evaluated before the IAA uses an outside expert?	• The independence and objectivity of the expert in respect to the engagement. • The relevant professional certifications and membership in a professional organization.

		• Experience and education in similar situations and the area in which they will be engaged. • Reputation. • Knowledge of the business and industry.
16.	What are examples of Engagements for which **outside service providers** may be needed?	Some of the types of engagements are: • Engagements that require specialist knowledge (such as tax questions, foreign languages, or IT) • Valuations of assets (both tangible and intangible) • Determination of physical amounts (for example, oil reserves) • Fraud • Interpretations of legal or tax matters • Mergers and acquisitions
17.	What is **Due Professional Care**?	Due professional care requires that **internal auditors apply the skill and care expected of a reasonably prudent and competent internal auditor**. Due Professional Care is needed in both assurance and consulting engagements.
18.	In Standard 1220, what must the internal auditor consider in **exercising** Due	The internal auditors must exercise due professional care by considering the: • The extent of work needed to achieve the engagement's objectives;

		Professional Care in Assurance Engagement?	• Relative complexity, materiality, or significance of matters to which assurance procedures are applied; • Adequacy and effectiveness of governance, risk management, and control processes; • Probability of significant errors, fraud, or noncompliance; and • Cost of assurance in relation to potential benefits. In exercising due professional care, internal auditors must **consider using technology-based audits and other data analysis techniques**. Internal **auditors must be alert to the significant risks that might affect objectives, operations, or resources**. However, assurance procedures alone, even when performed with due professional care, do not guarantee that all significant risks will be identified.
19.	In Standard 1220, what must the internal auditor consider in **exercising** Due Professional Care in Consulting Engagement?		Internal auditors **must exercise due professional care during a consulting engagement** by considering the: • **Needs and expectations of clients**, including the nature, timing, and communication of engagement results; • Relative complexity and extent of work needed to achieve the engagement's objectives; and • **Cost of the consulting engagement in relation to potential benefits.**

20.	What are the requirements of standard 1230 – Continuing Professional Development?	Internal auditors must enhance their knowledge, skills, and other competencies through continuing professional development.
21.	What does **continuing professional education** include?	It includes the: • Maintaining proficiency through continuing education. • Staying informed about improvements and current developments in the internal audit standards, procedures, and techniques.

SECTION C – PROFICIENCY AND DUE PROFESSIONAL CARE (WEIGHTAGE 18%)

TRUE / FALSE QUESTIONS AND ANSWERS

S.NO	QUESTIONS	ANSWERS
1.	There are ten competencies in the Competency Framework.	**TRUE.** Professional ethics, Internal audit management, IPPF, Governance risk and control, Business acumen, Communication, Persuasion and collaboration, Critical thinking, Internal audit delivery, Improvement and innovation.
2.	Proficiency is the ability to apply knowledge to situations likely to be encountered and deal with them appropriately without extensive recourse to technical research and assistance.	**TRUE.** The ability to apply **knowledge to situations** likely to be encountered and deal with them appropriately without extensive recourse to technical research and assistance.
3.	Understanding is the ability to apply broad knowledge to situations likely to be encountered, recognize significant deviations, and carry out the research	**TRUE.** The ability to apply **broad knowledge** to situations likely to be encountered, recognize significant deviations and carry out the research necessary to arrive at reasonable solutions.

	necessary to arrive at reasonable solutions.	
4.	Appreciation is the ability to recognize problems or potential problems and identify the additional research or assistance needed.	**TRUE.** The ability to **recognize** the existence of problems or potential problems and identify the additional research or assistance needed.
5.	Internal Auditors must have proficiency in Accounting, Economics, Commercial law, Taxation, Finance, Quantitative methods, Information technology, Risk management, Fraud	**FALSE.** Internal Auditors must have proficiency in applying **Internal audit standards, procedures, and techniques** in performing engagements.
6.	Internal Auditors must have an understanding of materiality, and significance of deviations from good business practices.	**TRUE.** Internal Auditors **must have** an understanding of the materiality and significance of deviations from good business practices.

7.	Internal Auditors must know to identify the indicators of fraud, and critical information technology risks and controls and available technology-based audit techniques.	**TRUE.** Internal Auditors **must know** To identify the indicators of fraud, and critical information technology risks and controls and available technology-based audit techniques.
8.	The Audit Committee is responsible for Proficiency and Due Professional Care of the Auditors.	**FALSE.** The **CAE** has this responsibility.
9.	The CAE can engage external specialists.	**TRUE.** If the IAA does not have the skills and competencies for an engagement, the CAE must either decline the engagement or go **outside the IAA or organization** to get those skills.
10.	Due professional care requires that internal auditors apply the skill and care expected of a prudent and competent internal auditor.	**FALSE.** Due professional care requires that internal auditors apply the skill and care expected of a **reasonably** prudent and competent internal auditor.
11.	Internal auditors must exercise due professional	**TRUE.** Internal auditors **must exercise due professional care during a consulting engagement** by considering the

	care during a consulting engagement	• **Needs and expectations of clients**, including the nature, timing, and communication of engagement results; • Relative complexity and extent of work needed to achieve the engagement's objectives; and • **Cost of the consulting engagement with potential benefits**.
12.	An understanding is required of internal auditors concerning accounting principles and techniques.	**FALSE.** Understanding **management principles** is required to recognize and evaluate the materially and significance of deviations from good business practices. An understanding means the ability to apply broad knowledge to situations likely to be encountered, recognize significant deviations, and be able to carry out the research necessary to arrive at reasonable solutions.
13.	Proficiency is required of internal auditors concerning internal auditing procedures and techniques.	**TRUE.** Proficiency in applying **internal auditing standards, procedures, and techniques** is required in performing engagements. Proficiency means the ability to apply knowledge to situations likely to be encountered and to deal with them without extensive recourse to technical research and assistance.
14.	Internal auditors should possess the ability to conduct training sessions in quantitative methods.	**FALSE.** The internal auditor is required only to appreciate **quantitative methods**, not have the ability to conduct training sessions, which would require a high degree of proficiency.
15.	An appreciation is required of	**TRUE.** An **appreciation** is required of the fundamentals of accounting, economics,

	internal auditors concerning Accounting principles and techniques.	commercial law, taxation, finance, quantitative methods, information technology, risk management, and fraud. An appreciation means the ability to recognize the existence of problems or potential problems and to identify the additional research to be undertaken or the assistance to be obtained.
16.	A primary reason for establishing an internal audit activity is to evaluate and improve the effectiveness of control processes.	**TRUE.** The internal audit activity helps an organization accomplish its objectives by bringing a **systematic, disciplined approach** to evaluating and improving the effectiveness of risk management, control, and governance processes (Definition of Internal Auditing).
17.	A formal code of ethics should reflect only legal standards of conduct for individuals and the organization.	**FALSE.** An ethical organization aspires to a **higher standard of behaviour** than mere legality.
18.	In complying with The IIA's Code of Ethics, an internal auditor should use individual judgment to apply the principles outlined in the Code.	**TRUE.** The IIA's Code of Ethics includes principles that internal auditors are expected to apply and uphold. They are interpreted by the Rules of Conduct, behaviour norms expected of internal auditors. That particular conduct is not mentioned in the Rules of Conduct does not prevent it from being unacceptable or discreditable. Consequently, a reasonable inference is that **individual judgment** is necessary to apply the **principles** and the **Rules of Conduct**.
19.	The Rules of Conduct in The	**TRUE.** The Rules of Conduct are an **essential component** of The IIA's Code of Ethics. There

Muhammad Zain

	IIA's Code of Ethics are intended to guide the ethical conduct of internal auditors.	are Rules of Conduct for each of the core principles of integrity, objectivity, confidentiality, and competency. The rules describe the behaviour expected of internal auditors. "These rules are an aid to interpreting the Principles into practical applications and are intended to guide the ethical conduct of internal auditors."
20.	An auditor who shall observe the law and make disclosures expected by the law is following the IIA's Code of Ethics Core Principle of Objectivity.	**FALSE.** The **integrity** of internal auditors establishes trust and thus provides the basis for reliance on their judgment. Rule of Conduct 1.2 under the integrity principle states, "Internal auditors shall observe the law and make disclosures expected by the law and the profession." Additionally, Rule of Conduct 1.3 states, "Internal auditors shall not knowingly be a party to any illegal activity or engage in acts that are discreditable to the profession of internal auditing or to the organization."

SECTION D – QUALITY ASSURANCE AND IMPROVEMENT PROGRAM (WEIGHTAGE 7%)

STUDY POINTS

S.No	Study Questions	Study Answers
1.	What does **QAIP** stand for?	Quality Assurance and Improvement Program
2.	What is the requirement of Standard 1300 – **Quality Assurance and Improvement Program**?	The chief audit executive must develop and maintain a quality assurance and improvement program covering all aspects of the internal audit activity.
3.	What is a **Quality Assurance and Improvement Program**?	Quality assurance and improvement programs are designed to evaluate the internal audit activity's conformance with the *Standards* and an evaluation of whether internal auditors apply the Code of Ethics. The program also assesses the efficiency and effectiveness of the internal audit activity and identifies opportunities for improvement. The chief audit executive should encourage board oversight in the quality assurance and improvement program.
4.	Explain the **purpose** of QAIP?	It enables an evaluation of: • Conformance with the Definition of Internal Auditing, the Code of Ethics, and the *Standards*. • The adequacy of the internal audit activity's charter, goals, objectives, policies, and procedures.

		• The contribution to the organization's governance, risk management, and control processes. • Completeness of coverage of the entire audit universe. • Compliance with applicable laws, regulations, and government or industry standards to which the internal audit activity may be subject. • The risks affecting the operation of the internal audit activity itself. • The effectiveness of continuous improvement activities and adoption of best practices. • Whether the internal audit activity adds value, improves the organization's operations, and contributes to the attainment of objectives."
5.	Who are the **stakeholders** of Internal Audit Activity?	The stakeholders of IAA include: • Board of directors • Senior management • External auditor • Operational managers • Customers • Shareholders • Regulators • Government
6.	How is QAIP **developed** and **implemented**?	The CAE should design the QAIP considering the size, nature, and structure of the IAA. • The role of internal audit management and staff in the quality process.

		• The activities that are covered through ongoing monitoring, periodic self-assessment, or external assessments. • The frequency of self-assessments and external assessments. • The level of quality, or maturity, desired by the internal audit activity and expected by its stakeholders.
7.	Which things are **evaluated** as part of QAIP?	The following things are evaluated as part of QAIP: • Conformance with the Definition of Internal Auditing, the Code of Ethics, and the Standards. • The adequacy of the internal audit activity's charter, goals, objectives, policies, and procedures. • The contribution to the organization's governance, risk management, and control processes. • Completeness of coverage of the entire audit universe. • Compliance with applicable laws, regulations, and government or industry standards to which the internal audit activity may be subject. • The risks affecting the operation of the internal audit activity itself. • The effectiveness of continuous improvement activities and adoption of best practices.

		• Whether the internal audit activity adds value, improves the organization's operations, and contributes to achieving objectives.
8.	At what **levels** QAIP is implemented?	The QAIP must be implemented and applied at three levels: 1. The individual internal audit engagement level (self-assessment at the audit, engagement, or operational level by the engagement supervisor, possibly a manager or the CAE) 2. The internal audit activity level (self-assessment at the internal audit activity or organizational level by the CAE), and 3. The external perspective (independent external assessment of the entire internal audit activity, including individual engagements by an internal/external assessor outside the internal audit function).
9.	What are the requirements of Standard 1310 – **Requirements of the Quality Assurance and Improvement Program**?	The quality assurance and improvement program **must include both internal and external assessments**.
10.	What are the two types of **internal assessments** in a QAIP?	The two types of internal assessments are: 1. **Ongoing internal assessments** of performance of the internal audit activity. 2. **Periodic internal assessments** of the program through self-assessment or from an independent person within the organization

		who is familiar with the internal auditing program.
11.	Elaborate on the **Ongoing Internal Assessments**?	**Ongoing Internal Assessments** are the conclusions and follow-up actions to ensure that improvements are implemented. Ongoing monitoring also helps the CAE assess the quality of the IAA's engagements. Ongoing reviews may be conducted through: • Supervision of the internal auditor's work during the audit engagement. • Checklists showing that processes adopted by the audit activity are being followed. • Peer review of work papers by auditors not involved in the engagement. • Feedback from audit customers and other stakeholders. • Analyses of performance metrics (for example, cycle time and recommendations accepted). • Project budgets, timekeeping systems, audit plan completion, and cost recoveries.
12.	Explain the **Periodic Self-Assessments**?	**Periodic Self-Assessments** should assess compliance with the activity's charter, the Definition of Internal Auditing, the Code of Ethics, and the *Standards*. This periodic self-assessment will evaluate: • The quality and supervision of the work performed.

		• The adequacy of the internal audit policies and procedures. • The ways in which the IAA adds value to the organization. • The progress towards achieving key performance indicators. • The degree to which stakeholder expectations have been met. Periodic internal self-assessment may: • Include more in-depth interviews and surveys of stakeholder groups. • Be performed by members of the IAA (that is, self-assessment). • Be performed by CIAs or other competent audit professionals currently assigned elsewhere in the organization. • Include self-assessment and preparation of materials subsequently reviewed by CIAs or other competent audit professionals from elsewhere in the organization. • Include benchmarking of the IAA practices and performance metrics against relevant best practices of the internal audit profession.
13.	What is the requirement of Standard 1312 – **External Assessments**?	External assessments must be conducted at least once every five years **by a qualified, independent assessor or assessment team from outside the organization**. The chief audit executive must discuss with the board:

		• The form and frequency of external assessment. • The qualifications and independence of the external assessor or assessment team, including any potential conflict of interest.
14.	How are **external assessments** accomplished?	External assessments may be accomplished through a full external assessment or a self-assessment with independent external validation. The external assessor must conclude conformance with the Code of Ethics and the *Standards*; the external assessment may also include operational or strategic comments.
15.	An **external assessor** will tend to focus on what items?	During the review, an external assessor will tend to focus on: • The adequacy of the internal audit charter. • The goals, objectives, policies, and procedures of the IAA. • Whether or not the IAA's work is in accordance with the charter. • Whether or not the work conforms with the Definition of Internal Auditing, the Code of Ethics, and the *Standards*. • The contribution of the IAA to the organization's risk management, governance, and internal controls. • The IAA's methods and work programs. • The skills and work performed by the individuals in the IAA.

		• Whether or not the IAA adds value and improves the operations of the organization.
16.	What are the two ways an **external assessment** may be done in a QAIP?	The two ways are: 1. A full external assessment is conducted by an external assessor or review team. 2. An independent assessor or review team can conduct an independent validation of the internal self-assessment and the corresponding report completed by the internal audit activity.
17.	To whom are the results of the **QAIP communicated**?	To senior management and the board of directors.
18.	How **often** should internal assessments be performed?	Ongoing assessments are performed throughout the year, and periodic assessments are performed as needed.
19.	How **often** should external assessments be performed?	At least once every five years.
20.	What are the requirements of Standard 1320 – **Reporting on the Quality Assurance and Improvement Program**?	**The chief audit executive must communicate the results of the quality assurance and improvement program to senior management and the board.** Disclosure should include: • The scope and frequency of both the internal and external assessments. • The qualifications and independence of the assessor(s) or assessment team, including potential conflicts of interest.

		• Conclusions of assessors. • Corrective action plans.
21.	When may the phrase "Conforms with the *International Standards for the Professional Practice of Internal Auditing*" **be used**?	It is used only if the results of the QAIP support it.
22.	To whom must **nonconformance** with the Standards be disclosed?	To senior management and the board.
23.	QAIP Assessments should include **evaluations of**?	QAIP assessments should include evaluations of: • Compliance with the Definition of Internal Auditing, the Code of Ethics, and the *Standards*, including timely corrective actions to remedy any significant instances of noncompliance. • Adequacy of the IAA's charter, goals, objectives, policies, and procedures. • Contribution to the organization's governance, risk management, and control processes. • Compliance with applicable laws, regulations, and other governmental or industry standards.

		• Effectiveness of continuous improvement activities and adoption of best practices.
		• The extent to which the internal auditing activity adds value and improves the organization's operations.

SECTION D – QUALITY ASSURANCE AND IMPROVEMENT PROGRAM (WEIGHTAGE 7%)

TRUE / FALSE QUESTIONS AND ANSWERS

S.NO	QUESTIONS	ANSWERS
1.	QAIP stands for Quality Assurance and Improvement Program	**TRUE.** QAIP stands for Quality Assurance and Improvement Program.
2.	The chief audit executive must develop and maintain a quality assurance and improvement program that covers some aspects of the internal audit activity.	**FALSE.** The chief audit executive must develop and maintain a quality assurance and improvement program covering **all** aspects of the internal audit activity.
3.	There are two types of Internal Assessments in QAIP.	**TRUE. Ongoing internal assessments** of the performance of the internal audit activity. **Periodic internal assessments** of the program through self-assessment or from an independent person within the organization who is familiar with the internal auditing program.
4.	Ongoing internal assessments are the results and follow-up actions to ensure that improvements are implemented.	**FALSE.** Ongoing internal assessments are the **conclusions** and follow-up actions to ensure that improvements are implemented. Ongoing monitoring also helps the CAE assess the quality of the IAA's engagements.

Muhammad Zain

	Ongoing monitoring also helps the CAE assess the quality of the IAA's engagements.	
5.	Periodic self-assessments may assess compliance with the activity's charter, the Definition of Internal Auditing, the Code of Ethics, and the *Standards*.	**FALSE.** Periodic self-assessments **should** assess compliance with the activity's charter, the Definition of Internal Auditing, the Code of Ethics, and the *Standards*.
6.	External assessments must be conducted at least annually by a qualified, independent assessor or assessment team from outside the organization.	**FALSE.** External assessments must be conducted at least once every **five** years by a qualified, independent assessor or assessment team from outside the organization.
7.	The results of QAIP is distributed to the members of the Internal Audit department.	**FALSE.** Results of QAIP is communicated To **senior management** and the **board of directors**.
8.	Ongoing assessments are performed on an annual basis.	**FALSE.** Ongoing assessments are performed **throughout the year**, and periodic assessments are performed as needed.

9.	Nonconformance with the Standards must be disclosed to the senior management and board.	**TRUE.** Nonconformance with the Standards must be **disclosed** to the **senior management** and **board**.
10.	Formal internal quality assessment of the internal audit activity (IAA) primarily serve the needs of the board of directors.	**FALSE.** Internal quality assessments primarily serve the needs of the **CAE**; however, they may also provide senior management and the board with an assessment of the IAA. The CAE needs assurance that the IAA complies with the Definition of Internal Auditing, the Code of Ethics and *Standards*.
11.	The interpretation related to the quality assurance given by the *Standards* is that External assessments can provide senior management and the board with independent assurance about the internal audit activity's quality.	**TRUE.** External assessments of an IAA contain an expressed opinion as to the entire spectrum of assurance and consulting work performed (or that should have been performed based on the internal audit charter) by the IAA, including its conformance with the Definition of Internal Auditing, the Code of Ethics, and the *Standards* and, as appropriate, includes recommendations for improvement. These assessments can have considerable value to the CAE and other members of the IAA, especially when benchmarking and best practices are shared.
12.	Ordinarily, those conducting internal quality program assessments should report to the board.	**FALSE.** The CAE establishes a structure for reporting results of internal assessments that maintain appropriate creditability and objectivity. Generally, those assigned responsibility for conducting ongoing and periodic reviews, report to the CAE while performing the reviews and communicates **results directly to the CAE**.

13.	External assessments can provide senior management and the board with independent assurance about the internal audit activity's quality.	**TRUE.** External assessments of an IAA contain an expressed opinion as to the entire spectrum of assurance and consulting work performed (or that should have been performed based on the internal audit charter) by the IAA, including its conformance with the Definition of Internal Auditing, the Code of Ethics, and the *Standards* and, as appropriate, includes recommendations for improvement. These assessments can have considerable value to the **CAE and other members of the IAA**, especially when **benchmarking and best practices** are shared.
14.	A chief audit executive shall recommend that the results of an external quality assessment be shared with the board	**TRUE.** By sharing the results of an external quality assessment with the board, the CAE is showing the **accountability** of the IAA to the board and being transparent about the results and effectiveness of the IAA as a whole.
15.	Internal auditors may report that their activities are conducted following the Standards only if an independent external assessment of the internal audit activity is conducted annually.	**FALSE.** According to Standard 1330-1, internal auditors may use the statement only if the assessment of the **quality improvement program** demonstrates that the **internal audit activity** complies with the Standards.
16.	The results of external assessments are communicated	**TRUE.** According to Standard 1320, the results of external assessments should be **communicated** upon their **completion**.

	upon their completion.	
17.	The CAE should meet with the board, with management present, to reinforce the independence of the internal audit activity.	**FALSE.** Private meetings between the CAE and the board **without management** present are an essential part of the functional reporting relationship.
18.	Freedom from conditions that threaten internal auditors' ability to do unbiased work avoids conflict of interest.	**FALSE. Independence** is "the freedom from conditions that threaten the ability of the internal audit activity to carry out internal audit responsibilities in an unbiased manner."
19.	Assessing the individual objectivity of internal auditors is the responsibility of the audit committee.	**FALSE.** The **CAE** must establish policies and procedures to assess the objectivity of individual internal auditors.
20.	A conflict of interest only exists when the internal auditor displays unethical behaviour or engages in improper acts.	**FALSE.** A conflict of interest exists even if no unethical or improper act results. The IIA Glossary defines conflict of interest as "any relationship that is, or appears to be, not in the best interest of the organization." Interpretation of Standard 1120, Conflict of Interest, states, "Conflict of interest is a situation in which an internal auditor, who is in a position of trust, has a competing professional or personal interest. Such competing interests can make it difficult to fulfill their duties impartially. A conflict of interest exists even if no unethical or improper act results. A conflict of interest

		can create an appearance of impropriety that can undermine confidence in the internal auditor, the internal audit activity, and the profession. A conflict of interest could impair an individual's ability to perform their duties and responsibilities objectively."
21.	Objectivity requires internal auditors not to subordinate their judgment on audit matters to that of others.	**TRUE.** Objectivity is "an **unbiased mental attitude** that allows internal auditors to perform engagements in such a manner that they believe in their work product and that no quality compromises are made. Objectivity requires that internal auditors do not subordinate their judgment on audit matters to others".
22.	When faced with an imposed scope limitation, the chief audit executive must refuse to perform the engagement until the scope limitation is removed.	**FALSE.** A scope limitation, along with its potential effect, needs to be **communicated to the board**.
23.	The internal audit activity collectively must possess or obtain specific competencies. Internal audit staff should be competent in general management principles.	**FALSE.** The internal audit activity collectively must possess or obtain the knowledge, skills, and other competencies needed to perform its responsibilities (Attr. Std. 1210). The emphasis of internal auditors' technical expertise is on (1) the IPPF, (2) governance, risk, and control, and (3) business acumen. For example, the internal audit staff and managers should demonstrate the appropriate use and interpretation of the **IPPF**.

24.	The skills of the internal audit staff are assessed semi-annually.	**FALSE.** The CAE should conduct periodic skills assessments to determine the specific resources available. Assessments should be performed at least **annually**.
25.	A company is planning to outsource the oversight of and responsibility for the internal audit activity.	**FALSE.** An organization may outsource none, some, or all of the functions of the internal audit activity. However, **oversight** of and **responsibility** for the internal audit activity **must not be outsourced**. As stated in Implementation Standard 1210.A1, "The chief audit executive must obtain competent advice and assistance if the internal auditors lack the knowledge, skills, or other competencies needed to perform all or part of the engagement."
26.	Practicing and non-practicing CIAs must complete 40 hours of continuing professional education (CPE) annually, including at least 2 hours of ethics training.	**FALSE.** CIAs demonstrate their continuing professional development by completing continuing professional education (CPE). **Practicing** and **non-practicing** CIAs must complete **40 hours** and **20 hours**, respectively, of CPE annually, including at least 2 hours of ethics training.
27.	Certified internal auditors may obtain CPE credits through performing internal audit engagements as a CAE.	**FALSE.** Qualifying CPE activities are those that contribute to internal audit competencies. They include educational programs, passing examinations, translating publications, authoring or contributing to publications, delivering oral presentations, participating as a subject matter expert volunteer, and performing external quality assessments. **Performing internal audit engagements as a CAE does not qualify as CPE.**

28.	Internal assessments of the internal audit activity consist of an independent assessment team that identifies areas for improvement.	**FALSE.** According to Implementation Guide 1310, "Internal assessments consist of **ongoing monitoring** and **periodic self-assessments**, which evaluate the internal audit activity's conformance with the mandatory elements of the IPPF, the quality and supervision of audit work performed, the adequacy of internal audit policies and procedures, the value the internal audit activity adds to the organization, and the establishment and achievement of key performance indicators." External assessments provide an opportunity for an independent assessment team to identify areas for improvement for the internal audit activity.
29.	Assessment of quality assurance and improvement program should include evaluation of the adequacy of the oversight of the work of external auditors.	**FALSE.** Oversight of the work of external auditors, including coordination with the internal audit activity, is the **board's responsibility**. It is not within the scope of the process for monitoring and assessing the QAIP.
30.	The chief audit executive should develop and maintain a quality assurance and improvement program that covers all aspects of the internal audit activity and continuously	**FALSE. Appraising** each internal auditor's work at least annually is properly a function of the human resources program of the internal audit activity.

	monitors its effectiveness, including Annual appraisals of individual internal auditors' performance.	
31.	External assessment of an internal audit activity is likely to evaluate a detailed cost-benefit analysis of the internal audit activity.	**FALSE.** The external assessment has a broad scope of coverage that includes (1) conformance with the Code of Ethics and the *Standards* evaluated by review of the internal audit activity's charter, plans, policies, procedures, practices, and applicable legislative and regulatory requirements; (2) the expectations of the internal audit activity expressed by the board, senior management, and operational managers; and (3) the efficiency and effectiveness of the internal audit activity (IG 1312). However, the **costs and benefits of internal auditing are neither easily quantifiable nor the subject of an external assessment.**
32.	A distinguishing feature of an external assessment is its objective to provide independent assurance.	**TRUE.** External assessments must be conducted at least once **every 5 years** by a qualified, independent reviewer or review team from outside the organization. Individuals who perform the external assessment are free of any obligation to, or interest in, the organization whose internal audit activity is assessed.
33.	The chief audit executive's disclosure to senior management and the board regarding the QAIP should	**FALSE.** Attribute Standard 1320, Reporting on the Quality Assurance and Improvement Program, states, "The chief audit executive must communicate the results of the quality assurance and improvement program to senior management and the board. Disclosure should include (1) the scope and frequency of both the internal and external

include checklists or automation tools used.	assessments; (2) the qualifications and independence of the assessor(s) or assessment team, including potential conflicts of interest; (3) conclusions of assessors; and (4) corrective action plans." **Checklists or automation tools used do not require disclosure.**

SECTION E – GOVERNANCE, RISK MANAGEMENT, AND CONTROL (WEIGHTAGE 35%)

STUDY POINTS

S.No	Study Questions	Study Answers
1.	What are the requirements of Standard 2100 – **Nature of Work**?	The internal audit activity must evaluate and contribute to improving the organization's governance, risk management, and control processes using a systematic, disciplined, and risk-based approach. Internal audit credibility and value are enhanced when auditors are proactive and their evaluations offer new insights and consider future impact.
2.	Explain the purpose of the **Three Lines Model**?	The Three Lines Model's purpose is to "help organizations identify **structures** and **processes** that best assist the achievement of objectives and **facilitate strong governance and risk management**."
3.	How many **parties** are there in the Three Lines Model?	There are four parties in the Three Lines Model: 1. **Management** takes actions to achieve organizational objectives, and this includes risk management. Management will perform both first-line roles and second-line roles. 2. **Internal Audit** provides independent assurance and performs third line roles. 3. **Governing Body** provides accountability to stakeholders for organizational oversight. The governing body will perform the governing body roles of integrity, leadership, and transparency.

		4. **External Assurance Providers** and provide additional assurance by satisfying legal and regulatory requirements and expectations that protect the interest of stakeholders, and they will also support and supplement internal sources of assurance when required by management.
4.	What are the Three Lines **roles**?	The three lines of roles are: 1. Provision of products and services to clients and managing risk. 2. Expertise, support, monitoring and challenge on risk-related matters. 3. Independent and objective assurance and advice on all matters related to the achievement of objectives.
5.	Define **Organizational Governance**?	Organizational Governance is defined as the combination of processes and structures implemented by the board to inform, direct, manage, and monitor the achievement of its objectives.
6.	What are the **cornerstones** of good Corporate Governance?	There are four cornerstones of good corporate governance. 1. The board of directors 2. Executive management 3. External auditors 4. Internal auditors Governance processes are strengthened when there is synergy among these four groups, enabling them to work well and productively.

7.	Who is an **independent director**, and how many should a company has?	A majority of the directors should be independent in both fact and appearance. An independent director has no current or prior professional or personal ties to the corporation or its management other than service as a director. Independent directors must be able and willing to be objective in their judgments.
8.	What is the requirement of Standard 2110 – **Governance**?	The internal audit activity must assess and make appropriate recommendations to improve the organization's governance processes for: • Making strategic and operational decisions. • Overseeing risk management and control. • Promoting appropriate ethics and values within the organization. • Ensuring effective organizational performance management and accountability. • Communicating risk and control information to appropriate areas of the organization. • Coordinating the activities of, and communicating information among, the board, external and internal auditors, other assurance providers, and management.
9.	Who is an **Audit Committee**?	An audit committee is a sub-component of the board of directors. It has various roles mainly overseeing the work of internal and external auditors.

10.	What is **Risk Management**?	A process to identify, assess, manage, and control potential events or situations to provide reasonable assurance regarding achieving the organization's objectives.
11.	On what **factors** is Risk dependent upon?	**Volatility** and **time** are two features that also impact risk. • **Volatility** refers to the **inconsistency of results**. For example, if sales fluctuate wildly from day to day, sales are highly **volatile**. Volatility increases the possibility of poor future results. • **Time** can also be a crucial element in risk. A project covering a more extended period is riskier than a project covering a shorter period.
12.	What are the requirements of Standard 2120 – **Risk Management**?	The internal audit activity must evaluate the effectiveness and contribute to the improvement of risk management processes.
13.	What are the **Three Lines of Defense**?	First Line: Operational Management Second Line: Risk Management and Compliance Functions Third Line: Internal Audit
14.	What are the major areas of **responsibility** of the board?	The major areas of responsibility of the board are: 1. Monitoring the CEO and other senior executives. 2. Overseeing the corporation's strategy and processes for managing the enterprise (including succession planning).

		3. Monitoring the corporation's risks and internal controls, including the ethical tone.
15.	What are **common committees** that the Board establishes?	1. Audit committee 2. Compensation committee 3. Governance committee Each committee should have a charter, authorized by the board, outlining how each will be organized, their duties and responsibilities, and how they report to the board. Each committee should be composed of independent directors only.
16.	Who are the **Stakeholders**?	A stakeholder is an individual or entity with a material interest in a company's achievements, validated through some form of investment, and thereby expects a benefit in return.
17.	Who are **Internal Stakeholders**?	Internal Stakeholders are: • Directors • Senior management • Employees • Trade unions or staff associations • Shareholders
18.	Who are **External Stakeholders**?	External Stakeholders are: • Customers • Suppliers • Contractors and subcontractors • Distribution networks • Communities • The general public and government

19.	What are **four levels** of relationships with stakeholders and what is each level based on?	Based on the stakeholder's interest and power, the company's relationship will be to: 1. **Ignore** the stakeholder (weak power, low interest) 2. Keep the stakeholder **informed** (weak power, high interest) 3. Keep the stakeholder **satisfied** (strong power, low interest) 4. Treat the stakeholder as a **key player** (strong power, strong interest)
20.	What is the **role of internal audit** in Corporate Governance?	The IAA must assess and make appropriate recommendations to improve the organization's governance processes for: • Making strategic and operational decisions. • Overseeing risk management and control. • Promoting appropriate ethics and values within the organization. • Ensuring effective organizational performance management and accountability. • Communicating risk and control information to appropriate areas of the organization. • Coordinating the activities of, and communicating information among, the board, external and internal auditors, other assurance providers, and management.

21.	What are the steps in auditing a company's **governance practices and structure**?	The steps are: 1. Understand the general principles and models of organizational governance. 2. Review existing governance-related documentation. 3. Develop a preliminary audit plan. 4. Meet with decision-makers (i.e., the board). 5. Execute the approved plan. 6. If necessary, consult legal counsel. 7. Complete the process, including a formal presentation to the board, and have essential decision-makers sign a "statement of acknowledgement."
22.	How is organizational culture **different** than organizational governance?	Organizational culture and its related practices are not written down or codified. Organizational culture can be rooted in the distinct personalities of company leadership or more generally in the ethnic, religious, or political context in which the business operates.
23.	What are the **six control environment** elements that organizational culture may impact?	The six control environments elements that impact organizational culture are: 1. Integrity and ethical values 2. Management's philosophy and operating style 3. Organizational structure 4. Assignment of authority and responsibility

		5. Human resource policies and practices
		6. Competence of personnel
24.	What is the internal auditor's role in assessing **Organizational Ethics**?	The internal audit activity must assess the design, implementation, and effectiveness of the organization's ethics-related objectives, programs, and activities.
25.	What does a **review** of organizational ethics focus on?	The review of organizational ethics focus on: 1. Policies, including the policy for reporting ethical violations 2. Procedures 3. Effectiveness 4. Disposition of ethical issues, including if the penalties are appropriately scaled if there is a consistent application, and if there is proper documentation. 5. Compliance
26.	What are **ethics advocates,** and who must act as an ethics advocate?	Ethics advocates are visible models of appropriate behaviour who encourage and support the code of conduct at all times and at all activity levels. Management **must** act as ethics advocates. All individuals in the company should be encouraged to be ethics advocates. Internal auditors are also key ethical advocates.

		The IIA Code of Ethics states that the internal auditors should exemplify the ethical behaviour that employees should practice.
27.	What is a **Code of Conduct**, and who is it applicable to?	A Code of Conduct, or Business Conduct Policy, outlines the specific behaviours required or prohibited for all employees. The Code of Conduct should be written in clear, concise language that eliminates ambiguity or contradictory interpretation. The Code of Conduct applies to all people in the organization, regardless of position, department, or length of employment.
28.	The code of conduct includes **guidance** on what topics?	The code of conduct includes guidance on the following topics: • Conflicts of interest – any conflict of interest may be disclosed to the company so that necessary steps can be taken on time. • Confidentiality of information – employees shall preserve confidential information. • Acceptance of gifts – employees must be restrained from accepting gifts of significant value from interested parties. • Compliance with all applicable laws, rules, and regulations – employees shall comply with all the laws, rules, and regulations. • Penalties – the Code must detail the consequences for any violations.
29.	What is the **role** of the IAA	The Code of Conduct needs to be periodically assessed by the IAA to ensure that it is relevant and reflects its needs. Additionally,

		with the Code of Conduct?	compliance with the Code of Conduct should also be tested periodically and may even be included in every engagement.
30.		What is **Corporate Social Responsibility**?	Corporate Social Responsibility is defined as the way firms integrate social, environmental, and economic concerns into their values, culture, decision-making, strategy, and operations in a transparent and accountable manner and thereby establish better practices within the firm, create wealth, and improve society.
31.		What are the **levels of responsibility** for CSR in a company?	• **The board** has overall responsibility for CSR. • **Management** is responsible for executing CSR and ensuring clear objectives, performance measurement, and reporting. • **Employees** must integrate CSR into their everyday activities. • **The internal auditors** should understand the risks and controls related to CSR and be responsible for auditing CSR.
32.		What are some of the **risks** associated with CSR?	Some of the risks associated with CSR are: • Reputation • Compliance • Liability and lawsuits • Operational • Company stock valuation • Employment market • Consumer sales • External business relationships
33.		What are the **seven core subjects** in ISO	The seven core subjects ISO 26000 are: 1. Organizational governance

	26000 – Guidance on Social Responsibility?	2. Human rights 3. Labor practices 4. The environment 5. Fair operating practices 6. Consumer issues 7. Community involvement and development
34.	What are the **five main** aspects of CSR in ISO 26000?	The five main aspects of CSR according to ISO 26000 are: 1. A company should operate ethically and with integrity. 2. A company should treat its employees fairly and with respect. 3. A company should demonstrate respect for human rights. 4. A company should be a responsible citizen in its community. 5. A company should do what it can to sustain the environment for future generations.
35.	What are the **four levels** of the pyramid of social responsibility?	The four levels of the pyramid of social responsibility are: 1. Philanthropic responsibilities – be a good corporate citizen 2. Ethical responsibilities – be ethical 3. Legal responsibilities – obey the law 4. Economic responsibilities – be profitable and sustainable
36.	What are the **seven steps** in	The steps in CSR process are:

	the CSR Process?	**1. Set priorities and policies** for areas such as ethics, labour, the environment, charity, and any other relevant CSR areas. **2. Set specific objectives and strategies** to achieve the policies set by management. **3. Communicate and embed CSR** into controls and decision-making. **4. Track the activities related to CSR** so that the results of the CSR policies and objectives can be measured, analyzed, and benchmarked. **5. Engage stakeholders** to resolve any complaints and receive feedback on the CSR issues affecting them. **6. Audit results**, including controls related to CSR and any public disclosures. **7. Report results**.
37.	What are **different approaches** that can be taken to auditing CSR?	• **By element** – governance, ethics, environment, transparency, HSE, and human rights. • **By stakeholder or stakeholder group.** • **By subject.** For example, by workplace, marketplace, environment, and community. • **By department/function.** Audit CSR separately for each department within the organization. • **By third party.** Audit third parties for compliance with CSR terms and conditions.

38.	What are the **elements** of CSR that are commonly audited?	The elements are CSR that are commonly audited are: • Governance – are board members fulfilling their roles and responsibilities. • Ethics – are there policies and procedures for reporting ethical issues. • Environment – are safeguards to an environment in place. • Transparency – are the activities of organization clear and un ambiguous. • Healthy, Safety, and Security – are health and safety measures being incorporated. • Human Rights and Work Conditions – are employees being fairly compensated, and a proper work environment is given.
39.	What are the **stakeholder groups** in auditing CSR?	• Employees and their families – are employees satisfied with the remuneration and benefits system of the company. • Environmental organizations – which environmental agencies shall have input. • Customers – are customers provided the desired products and services, and their information is kept confidential. • Suppliers – are suppliers paid on time. • Communities – does the company involve in charity and volunteering activities. • Shareholders – is the shareholders' wealth being maximized.

40.	Define **Risk**?	The possibility of an event occurring will have an impact on the achievement of objectives. Risk is measured in terms of impact and likelihood. It can also be defined as any event or action that can keep an organization from achieving its objectives.
41.	Define **Risk Management**?	Risk management is defined as a process to identify, assess, manage, and control potential events or situations to provide reasonable assurance regarding the organization's objectives.
42.	What is the requirement of Standard 2120 – **Risk Management**?	The internal audit activity must evaluate the effectiveness and contribute to the improvement of risk management processes.
43.	What is the Internal Auditor's responsibility relating to risk management in **consultancy engagements**?	During consulting engagements, internal auditors must address risks consistent with the engagement's objectives and be alert to the existence of other significant risks. Internal auditors must incorporate knowledge of risks gained from consulting engagements into their evaluation of the organization's risk management processes. When assisting management in establishing or improving risk management processes, internal auditors must refrain from assuming any management responsibility by managing risks.
44.	What are two factors on which	Risk is dependent on two factors.

	risk is **dependent upon**?	1. Volatility – refers to the inconsistency of results. It increases the probability of poor results. 2. Time – higher the time, the riskier the project or activity is.
45.	What are the **four broad categories** of risk?	The four broad categories of risk are: 1. Strategic risks – affect the whole organization. 2. Operational risks – results from inadequate or failed internal processes, people, or systems. 3. Financial risks – relates to the financial performance of the company. 4. Hazard risks – arises from natural disasters, injuries, and accidents at the company's premises.
46.	What is **risk capacity**?	Risk capacity is the maximum amount of risk that an organization can tolerate without irreparably damaging the company.
47.	What is **risk appetite**?	Risk appetite is defined in the IIA Glossary as "the level of risk that an organization is willing to accept." Risk appetite is shaped by stakeholders' expectations, regulatory and contractual requirements, and the influence of technology, capital, and human resources.
48.	What is **risk tolerance**?	Risk tolerance is the amount of variance in the returns from an activity that a company is willing to tolerate.

		The higher the risk tolerance, the **greater the range of outcomes a company is willing to accept**.
49.	What are some factors that **influence** a company's **risk appetite**?	The factors that influence a company's risk appetite are: • Their position in the business-development cycle – startup company needs a high-risk appetite. • The viewpoints of the major stakeholders – banks prefer lower risk appetite, and shareholders prefer aggressive actions. • Accounting factors – volume and complexity of transactions, frequent changes in laws and regulations. • The opportunity for fraud – the low likelihood of fraud will increase the risk appetite. • Entity-level factors – the personnel, changes in the organization's structure, and changes in key personnel. • External factors – changes in the economy, industry, or technology can affect risk appetite. • Governmental restrictions – affects the company's activities and thus risk appetite.
50.	What are the **five steps** in the risk management process?	The five steps in the risk management process are: 1. Risk identification 2. Risk assessment 3. Risk prioritization

		4. Response planning 5. Risk monitoring
51.	What are some **event identification** techniques?	The examples of event identification techniques are: • Brainstorming sessions • Event inventories and loss event data • Interviews and self-assessment • Facilitated workshops • SWOT analysis • Risk questionnaires and risk surveys • Scenario analysis • Technology
52.	What is **Inherent Risk**?	Inherent risk is defined as "the level of risk that resides with an event or process prior to management taking a mitigation action." It is the amount of risk that occurs naturally in the activities of the company. Management cannot do anything about the **existence** of inherent risk; however, it can take steps to address and, where appropriate, mitigate its **effects**.
53.	What is **Residual Risk**?	Residual risk is defined as: "The level of risk that remains after management has taken action to mitigate the risk." Residual Risk = Inherent risk – activities of management to address the risk.
54.	What two factors are used to assess the **risk exposure**?	The factors are: 1. Loss frequency or probability 2. Loss severity
55.	What is a **Risk Map**?	A visual depiction of relative risks based on their expected frequency and expected loss.

56.	What are the six quantitative **risk assessment tools**?	The quantitative risk assessment tools are:
		1. Value at Risk (VaR) measures the potential loss in value of a risky asset as the result of a specific risk event over a defined period for a given confidence interval. VaR is based on the assumption that the possible outcome of the event is represented by a normal distribution or bell curve.
		2. Cash Flow at Risk measures the likelihood that cash flows will drop by more than a certain amount over a given time. Expected cash flows are tested for their sensitivity to certain risks. Cash Flow at Risk uses the measures of a normal distribution.
		3. Earnings at Risk measures the confidence interval for a fall in earnings during a specific period by examining how earnings vary around expected earnings. Variables are examined to determine their effect on earnings, such as a 1% movement in interest rates would have on earnings.
		4. Earnings Distributions is a graphical representation of the probability distribution of various potential levels of return.
		5. Earnings Per Share Distributions is a graphical representation of the probability distribution of various potential amounts of earnings per share (EPS).
		6. Benchmarking compares the company's risk profile and the impact of potential risks with those of similar companies.

Muhammad Zain

57.	What are the **four measures** of potential loss?	The four measures of potential loss are: 1. Expected loss 2. Unexpected loss 3. Maximum probable loss 4. Maximum possible loss (also called extreme or catastrophic loss)
58.	What is the **expected loss**?	The amount that management expects to lose to a given risk per year on average over several years. Because the loss is expected, it should be included in the budget.
59.	What is the **unexpected loss**?	The amount that could likely be lost to the risk event in an awful year, more than the amount budgeted for the expected loss, up to the maximum probable loss. The business should reserve the unexpected loss amount as capital.
60.	What is the **maximum probable** loss?	The most significant loss that can occur under foreseeable circumstances. Damage greater than the maximum probable loss could occur, but, in the judgment of management, it is doubtful to occur.
61.	What is the **maximum possible** loss?	The worst-case scenario. It represents the greatest possible loss from a specific risk or event.
62.	What are the **five responses** to risk?	The five responses to risk are: 1. Avoiding or eliminating the risk 2. Reducing or mitigating the risk 3. Transferring or sharing the risk 4. Retaining the risk

		5. Exploiting or accepting the risk
63.	What are the **benefits** of Risk Management?	Risk management provides the following benefits: • Increasing shareholder value through minimizing losses and maximizing opportunities. • Fewer disruptions to operations. • Better utilization of resources. • Fewer shocks and unwelcome surprises. • Employees, other stakeholders, and relevant governing and regulatory bodies are more confident in the organization. • More effective strategic planning. • Better cost control. • Timelier assessment of and grasp of new opportunities. • Better and more complete contingency planning. • Improved ability to meet objectives and take advantage of opportunities.
64.	What is **Enterprise Risk Management**?	Enterprise risk management is the culture, capabilities, and practices that organizations **integrate with strategy-setting** and apply when they carry out that strategy, to manage risk in **creating, preserving, and realizing value**.

65.	What are the **five components** of the COSO ERM Framework?	The components of the COSO ERM framework are: 1. Governance and culture 2. Strategy and objective-setting 3. Performance 4. Review and revision 5. Information, communication, and reporting
66.	What are the **principles** of the "governance and culture" component of ERM?	The principles of the governance and culture component of ERM are: 1. Exercises board oversight 2. Establishes operating structure 3. Defines desired culture 4. Demonstrates commitment to core values 5. Attracts, develops and retains capable individuals
67.	What are the **principles** of the "strategy and objective setting" component of ERM?	The principles are: 1. Analyzes business context 2. Defines risk appetite 3. Evaluate alternative strategies 4. Formulates business objectives
68.	What are the **principles** of the "performance"	1. Identifies risk 2. Assesses severity of risk

	component of ERM?	3. Prioritizes risks 4. Implements risk responses 5. Develops portfolio view
69.	What are the **principles** of the "review and revision" component of ERM?	1. Assesses substantial change 2. Reviews risk and performance 3. Pursues improvement in enterprise risk management
70.	What are the **principles** of the "information, communication and reporting" component of ERM?	1. Leverages information systems 2. Communicates risk information 3. Reports on risk, culture, and performance
71.	What are the three areas of **principles and guidance** in ISO 31000?	The three areas of principles and guidance in ISO 31000: **1. Principles.** The interrelated values are foundational to the risk-management process. **2. Framework.** How the risk-management plan should be integrated into "significant activities and functions." **3. Process.** A step-by-step list of procedures to design and execute risk management.
72.	What are the **eight principles** that ISO 31000 sets forth to guide risk-	1. Integrated – risk management shall be an integral part of business functions. 2. Structured and comprehensive – risk management shall be structured.

	management procedures?	3. Customized – the process must be designed to accommodate the specific needs of the organization. 4. Inclusive – all stakeholders are involved in risk management. 5. Dynamic – risk management process shall be adaptable and change when required. 6. Best available information – risk management shall run according to the best available information. 7. Human and cultural factors – risk management shall accommodate the human and cultural factors in the process. 8. Continual improvement – risk management is an ongoing process.
73.	What are the **six steps** of the risk-management process in ISO 31000?	The six steps of the risk management process in ISO 31000 are: 1. Communication and consultation 2. Scope, context, and criteria 3. Risk assessment 4. Risk treatment 5. Monitoring and review 6. Recording and reporting
74.	What is the **role of the IAA** in the risk-	The internal audit activity must evaluate the effectiveness and contribute to the improvement of risk management processes.

	management process?	Determining whether risk management processes are effective is a judgment resulting from the internal auditor's assessment that: • Organizational objectives support and align with the organization's mission. • Significant risks are identified and assessed. • Appropriate risk responses are selected that align risks with the organization's risk appetite. • Relevant risk information is captured and communicated promptly across the organization, enabling staff, management, and the board to carry out their responsibilities. • The internal audit activity may gather the information to support this assessment during multiple engagements. The results of these engagements, when viewed together, provide an understanding of the organization's risk management processes and their effectiveness. Risk management processes are monitored through ongoing management activities, separate evaluations, or both.
75.	What must an assessment of the risk-management process **address**?	The internal auditor must be satisfied that the organization's risk management processes address: 1. Risks that arise from business strategies and activities are identified and prioritized. 2. Management and the board set the level of risk acceptable to the organization (assess risk appetite).

		3. Risk mitigation or reduction activities are designed and implemented to reduce or otherwise manage risk at acceptable levels. 4. Risk is periodically reassessed on an ongoing basis. 5. Reports are given periodically to the board and management on the risk assessment process.
76.	How is evidence for risk-management assessments **gathered**?	Evidence to support the risk assessment is usually obtained from engagements throughout the year. Because there is no formula to follow, the successful assessment of risk often rests with the professional judgment and experience of the internal auditors and the CAE.
77.	What should the IAA do when there is no **risk-management process**?	The CAE must convince the board and senior management to establish one, even with an informal set of procedures.
78.	In what three areas should the IAA provide assurance about the **effectiveness** of risk management?	1. The design and implementation of the risk management processes. 2. Identification of critical risks and the effectiveness of their controls. 3. Assessment and reporting of risk and controls.
79.	What are consulting engagements connected to risk	• Giving assurance on the risk management process • Giving assurance that risks are correctly evaluated

	management that are **core roles** of the IAA?	• Evaluating risk management processes • Evaluating the reporting of key risks • Reviewing the management of key risks
80.	What are consulting engagements connected to risk management that are **legitimate roles** of the IAA?	• Facilitating the identification and evaluating risks • Coaching management in responding to risks • Coordinating ERM activities • Consolidated reporting on risks • Maintaining and developing the ERM framework • Championing the establishment of ERM • Developing the ERM strategy for board approval
81.	What are consulting engagements connected to risk management that the IAA **should not undertake**?	• Setting the risk appetite • Imposing risk management processes • Management assurance on risks • Taking decisions on risk responses • Implementing responses on management's behalf • Accountability for risk management

82.	How does the IIA Glossary define **Control**?	"Any action taken by management, the board, and other parties to manage risk and increase the likelihood that established objectives and goals will be achieved. Management plans, organizes, and directs the performance of sufficient actions to provide reasonable assurance that objectives and goals will be achieved."
83.	Internal control provides reasonable assurance about the achievement of objectives in what **three areas**?	1. Operations – effectiveness and efficiency 2. Reporting – reliable financial reporting 3. Compliance – adherence to laws and regulations
84.	What are the **five types** of controls?	The five types of controls are: 1. Directive 2. Preventive 3. Detective 4. Corrective 5. Compensating
85.	Explain the **Directive Controls**?	To **cause** or **encourage** a desirable event to occur. For example: • Policies and procedures put in place by executive management. • Management directives, such as directing all internal auditors to be CIAs. • Making sure employees have job descriptions.

86.	Explain the **Preventive Controls**?	To **avoid** the occurrence of an unwanted event. These are key controls for events that would be very harmful to the company if they occurred. For example: • Segregation of duties. • Suitable authorization of transactions. • Checking creditworthiness of customers before goods are shipped. • Physical controls to safeguard assets such as equipment, inventories, securities, cash, and so forth. • These may also be "yes/no" controls that check if a specific condition exists or not.
87.	Explain the **Detective Controls**?	To **detect** undesirable events that have occurred. It can be used to detect events that could harm the company if not corrected. For example: • Bank reconciliations. • Checking for missing document numbers in pre-numbered documents. • Performance reporting with variances.
88.	Explain the **Corrective Controls**?	To **correct** undesirable events that have already occurred.

		For example, procedures are put in place to remedy problems discovered by detective controls, such as steps taken to identify the cause and modify the processing system to minimize future occurrences of the problem.
89.	Explain the **Compensating Controls**?	To **compensate** for weaknesses in the control system. These reduce risk when other controls are not effective but not sufficient by themselves to control risks. For example, • Bank reconciliation (also a detective control). • Additional independent oversight.
90.	What are the **three timings** of controls?	1. Feedforward controls 2. Concurrent controls 3. Feedback controls
91.	What are **Feedforward controls**?	**Feedforward controls** identify a problem before it occurs and attempt to prevent it from occurring. An example of feedforward controls is preventive maintenance on a machine to avoid a breakdown. Policies and procedures are other examples of feedforward controls.
92.	What are **Concurrent Controls?**	**Concurrent controls** operate simultaneously as they monitor and make adjustments based upon immediate feedback from the system.
93.	What are **Feedback Controls**?	**Feedback controls** identify a problem after it has occurred. Although this may be the most common form of control, it is the least effective and least efficient because time and money have been wasted before detection.

94.	What are the characteristics of **effective controls**?	An effective control system should have the following characteristics: • **Economical.** There must be a positive cost/benefit ratio, meaning the organization saves more than the control cost. • **Meaningful.** Only significant, material items need controls. • **Appropriate.** The control system should relate to an objective or goal of the company. • **Congruent.** The result of the system should be helpful and in line with what it is measuring. • **Timely.** The information must be available in enough time to act upon it. • **Simple.** The control must be understandable to the people using it. • **Operational.** The control should provide benefits to operations and not simply be interesting.
95.	What are the **limitations** of Internal controls?	The limitations of Internal Controls are: 1. Internal controls can provide only **reasonable assurance** that objectives can be achieved. Internal controls should never be promoted as a guarantee. 2. Human error, faulty judgment, **collusion**, and fraud can all limit the effectiveness of controls.

		3. Excessive or unreasonable controls can increase bureaucracy and reduce productivity. Controls must be evaluated in terms of their **cost** and **benefit** to avoid wasting resources.
96.	Who is **responsible** for Internal controls?	The **board of directors oversees** the control system. The **CEO** is responsible for the "**tone at the top**." **Senior managers delegate responsibility** for establishing specific internal control policies and procedures. **Financial officers and their staffs** are central to the exercise of control. **Internal auditors** play a monitoring role. Virtually **all employees** are involved in internal control. **External parties such as independent auditors** often provide valuable information for effective internal control.
97.	What are the three **main elements** of the control process?	The three main elements of the control process are: 1. Setting the objectives. 2. Measuring performance against a standard. 3. Evaluating the results then correcting or regulating the performance.
98.	What are **input controls** in an automated control system?	Input Controls in an automated control system are: 1. Edit checks

		2. Key verifications 3. Redundancy checks 4. Echo checks 5. Completeness checks
99.	What are **Edit Checks**?	**Edit checks** confirm the validity and accuracy of input data, such as verifying that each field has the proper numeric, alphabetic, or alphanumeric format and that the information in the transaction is reasonable.
100.	What are **Key Verifications**?	**Key verification** is the requirement of inputting information again and comparing the two inputs. For example, entering a new password twice before it is saved.
101.	What are **Redundancy Checks**?	**Redundancy checks** send additional sets of data to confirm the accuracy and validity of the original data.
102.	What are **Echo Checks**?	**Echo checks** send data back to the sender to compare it with what was originally sent.
103.	What are **Completeness Checks**?	**Completeness checks** (for transmission of data) determine whether all necessary information has been sent.
104.	What are **processing controls** in an automated control system?	The processing controls in an automated control system are: 1. Posting checks 2. Cross-footing 3. Zero balance checks 4. Run-to-run control totals 5. Internal header and trailer labels 6. Concurrency controls 7. Key integrity checks
105.	Define the **Posting Checks**?	**Posting checks** compare the contents of the record before and after updating.

106.	What is **Cross-Footing**?	**Cross-footing** compares the sum of the individual components to the total figure.
107.	What are **Zero Balance Checks**?	**Zero balance checks** are used when a total sum should be 0.
108.	What are **Run-to-run control totals**?	**Run-to-run control totals** verify the data values during the different processing stages and help ensure the completeness of all transactions.
109.	What are **Internal Header** and **Trailer Labels**?	**Internal header** and **trailer labels** ensure that the correct files are processed.
110.	What are **Concurrency Controls**?	**Concurrency controls** manage two or more programs trying to access the same information at the same time.
111.	What are **Key Integrity Checks**?	**Key integrity checks** ensure that the keys (characteristics of records that allow them to be sorted) are not changed during data processing.
112.	What are **output controls** in an automated control system?	Output controls in an automated control system are: 1. Output distribution controls 2. Output retention controls 3. Forms controls 4. Error logs
113.	Explain the **Output Distribution Controls**?	**Output distribution controls** ensure that distribution is made following pre-authorized automated or manual parameters.
114.	What is **Output Retention Controls**?	**Output retention controls** ensure that output is retained following organizational policies, considering statutory and legal requirements.

115.	What are **Forms Controls**?	**Forms controls** make sure that there is proper control over checks, bonds, and stock certificates. These items need to be protected by physical and logical controls.
116.	What are **Error Logs**?	**Error logs** are listings of processing errors. These error logs need to be reviewed to ensure that data is still being correctly processed.
117.	What **four duties** should always be segregated?	The following duties shall always be segregated. 1. **Authorizing** a transaction. 2. **Recording** the transaction, preparing source documents, and maintaining journals. 3. Keeping **physical custody** of the related asset. For example, receiving checks in the mail. 4. The **periodic reconciliation** of the physical assets to the recorded amounts for those assets.
118.	What is the **collusion**?	Collusion is when two or more people work together to get around the controls that are in place.
119.	What are the **five components** of internal control?	The five components of Internal Control are: 1. Control environment 2. Risk assessment 3. Control activities 4. Information and communication 5. Monitoring activities

120.	What is the **Control Environment** in the COSO Model?	The control environment sets the tone for the organization, influencing the control consciousness of its people. The control environment is the foundation for the other components of internal control.
121.	What is **Risk Assessment** in the COSO Model?	The risk assessment identifies and analyzes relevant risks to achieving objectives and forms a basis for managing risks.
122.	What are **Control Activities** in the COSO Model?	Control activities ensure that management directives are carried out. These policies and procedures also outline the necessary steps to address risks to the organization's objectives.
123.	What are **Information and Communication** in the COSO Model?	These are the systems or processes that support the identification, capture, and exchange of information in a form and time frame that enable people to carry out their responsibilities.
124.	What is **Monitoring** in the COSO Model?	These are processes used to assess the quality of internal control performance over time. This objective is accomplished through ongoing monitoring activities, separate evaluations, or a combination of the two.
125.	What are the five principles of the **Control Environment** under the COSO Model?	The five principles of Control Environment under the COSO model are: 1. The organization demonstrates a commitment to integrity and ethical values. 2. The board of directors demonstrates independence from management and exercises oversight of the development and performance of internal control. 3. Management establishes, with board oversight, structures, reporting lines, and

		appropriate authorities and responsibilities to pursue objectives.
		4. The organization demonstrates a commitment to attract, develop, and retain competent individuals aligned with objectives.
		5. The organization holds individuals accountable for their internal control responsibilities in the pursuit of objectives.
126.	What are the **four principles** of Risk Assessment under the COSO Model?	The four principles of Risk Assessment under the COSO Model are: 1. The organization specifies objectives with sufficient clarity to identify and assess risks relating to objectives. 2. The organization identifies risks to achieve its objectives across the entity and analyzes risks as a basis for determining how the risks should be managed. 3. The organization considers the potential for fraud in assessing risks to the achievement of objectives. 4. The organization identifies and assesses changes that could significantly impact the system of internal control.
127.	What are the three principles of the **Control Activities** under the COSO Model?	The three principles of Control Activities under the COSO model are: 1. The organization selects and develops control activities that contribute to the mitigation of risks to achieve objectives to acceptable levels.

		2. The organization selects and develops general control activities over technology to support the achievement of objectives. 3. The organization deploys control activities through policies that establish expectations and procedures that put policies into action.
128.	What are the **three principles** of Information and Communication under the COSO Model?	1. The organization obtains or generates, and uses relevant, quality information to support the functioning of internal control. 2. The organization internally communicates information, including objectives and responsibilities for internal control, necessary to support the functioning of internal control. 3. The organization communicates with external parties regarding matters affecting the functioning of internal control.
129.	What are the two principles of **Monitoring activities** under the COSO Model?	1. The organization selects, develops, and performs ongoing and separate evaluations to ascertain whether the components of internal control are present and functioning. 2. The organization evaluates and communicates internal control deficiencies promptly to those parties responsible for taking corrective action, including senior management and the board of directors, as appropriate.
130.	What type of **controls** do both COSO and CoCo emphasize?	**Soft controls** emphasize ideas and expectations (for example, shared values, expectations, commitment, competence, and trust) rather than specific tasks (for example, policies and procedures).

131.	What are the **key tenets** of the Turnbull Report?	• Board's responsibility for internal controls • Management's responsibility for internal controls • Employees' responsibility for internal controls • Adopting a risk-based approach • Ongoing monitoring of risks and controls
132.	What is the role of the IAA in the **company's control system**?	The internal audit activity must assist the organization in maintaining effective controls by evaluating their effectiveness and efficiency and promoting continuous improvement.
133.	What are the steps in the evaluation of the **effectiveness** of controls?	The steps in the evaluation of the effectiveness of controls are: 1. Identify objectives and any associated risks. 2. Determine the significance of any risks. 3. Make note of the responses to these risks. 4. Identify the "key controls." 5. Assess how well a given control is designed. 6. Test the control to ascertain the effectiveness of the design.
134.	What three criteria can help the IAA measure the **effectiveness** of	1. The level of control must be "appropriate for the risk it addresses." For example, petty cash does not need as many controls as cash received from customers.

a specific control?	2. The costs of the control must not exceed the benefits it provides. For example, the office supply cabinet does not need 24/7 surveillance and a biometric scanner for access, but a server room certainly would. 3. No control should "create significant business concerns." For example, regardless of how efficiently a control manages a particular risk if the control breaks the law, it puts the company in significant legal jeopardy.

SECTION E – GOVERNANCE, RISK MANAGEMENT, AND CONTROL (WEIGHTAGE 35%)

TRUE / FALSE QUESTIONS AND ANSWERS

S.No	Questions	Answers
1.	Risk is defined as the probability of an event occurring that will impact the achievement of objectives.	**FALSE.** Risk is defined as the **possibility** of an event occurring that will impact the achievement of objectives.
2.	A process to identify, assess, manage, and control potential events or situations to provide limited assurance regarding the achievement of the organization's objectives.	**FALSE.** Risk Management is A process to identify, assess, manage, and control potential events or situations to provide **reasonable** assurance regarding achieving the organization's objectives.
3.	Risk is dependent on three factors.	**FALSE. Volatility** and **time** are two features that also impact risk.
4.	The internal audit activity must evaluate the efficiency and contribute to the improvement of risk management processes.	**FALSE.** The internal audit activity must evaluate the **effectiveness** and contribute to the improvement of risk management processes.

Muhammad Zain

5.	Organizational Governance is defined as the combination of processes and procedures implemented by the board to inform, direct, manage, and monitor the achievement of its objectives.	**FALSE.** Organizational Governance is defined as the combination of processes and **structures** implemented by the board to inform, direct, manage, and monitor the achievement of its objectives.
6.	The cornerstones of good corporate governance are the BOD, Management, External and Internal Auditors.	**TRUE.** The cornerstones of good corporate governance are the **BOD**, **Management**, **External** and **Internal Auditors**.
7.	Few of the directors should be independent in both fact and appearance.	**FALSE.** A **majority** of the directors should be independent in both fact and appearance.
8.	An independent director has current or prior professional or personal ties to the corporation or its management other than service as a director.	**FALSE.** An independent director has **no** current or prior professional or personal ties to the corporation or its management other than service as a director.
9.	Independent directors must be able and	**TRUE.** Independent directors must be able and willing to be objective in their **judgments**.

	willing to be objective in their judgments.	
10.	Can a company ignore the stakeholders who have weak power and low interest?	**TRUE. Ignore** the stakeholder (weak power, low interest)
11.	Is it necessary to keep informed the stakeholders who have weak power but high interest?	**TRUE.** Keep the stakeholder **informed** (weak power, high interest)
12.	Satisfaction is necessary for strong power but low-interest stakeholders?	**TRUE.** Keep the stakeholder **satisfied** (strong power, low interest)
13.	A key player is the category of stakeholders with strong power and strong interest?	**TRUE.** Treat the stakeholder as a **key player** (strong power, strong interest)
14.	Do the IAA make strategic and operational decisions?	**FALSE.** It is the responsibility of the **Board of Directors and Management**. IAA only assess and make appropriate recommendations to improve the organization's governance process.
15.	Management is responsible for promoting appropriate ethics and values within the organization.	**TRUE.** It is the responsibility of the management.

16.	Organizational culture and its related practices are written down or codified.	**FALSE.** Organizational culture and its related practices are **not written down** or **codified**.
17.	The internal audit activity must assess the design, implementation, and effectiveness of the organization's ethics-related objectives, programs, and activities.	**TRUE.** It is the responsibility of the IAA.
18.	Management may act as ethics advocates.	**FALSE.** Management **must** act as ethics advocates.
19.	The Code of Conduct should be written in clear, concise language that eliminates ambiguity or contradictory interpretation.	**TRUE.** The Code of Conduct should be written in **clear**, **concise language** that eliminates ambiguity or contradictory interpretation.
20.	A Code of Conduct, or Business Conduct Policy, outlines the general behaviours required or	**FALSE.** A Code of Conduct, or Business Conduct Policy, outlines the **specific** behaviours required or prohibited for all employees.

	prohibited for all employees.	
21.	The Code of Conduct applies to tactical and operational people in the organization.	**FALSE.** The Code of Conduct applies to **all people in the organization**, regardless of position, department, or length of employment.
22.	Risk is defined as the reasonable certainty of an event occurring that will impact the achievement of objectives. Risk is measured in terms of impact and likelihood."	**FALSE.** Risk is the **possibility** of an event occurring that will have an impact on the achievement of objectives. Risk is measured in terms of impact and likelihood."
23.	Risk capacity is the minimum amount of risk that an organization can tolerate without irreparably damaging the company.	**FALSE.** Risk capacity is the **maximum amount of risk** that an organization can tolerate without irreparably damaging the company.
24.	Risk Appetite is defined as the level of risk that an organization is not willing to accept."	**FALSE.** Risk Appetite is defined as the level of risk that an organization is **willing to accept**."
25.	Risk tolerance is the amount of variance in the returns from an activity that a company is	**TRUE.** Risk tolerance is the amount of **variance** in the returns from an activity that a company is **willing to tolerate**.

Muhammad Zain

	willing to tolerate.	
26.	The higher the risk tolerance, the lower the range of outcomes a company is willing to accept.	**FALSE.** The higher the risk tolerance, the **greater** the range of outcomes a company is willing to accept.
27.	Residual risk is defined as: "The level of risk that remains after management has taken action to mitigate the risk."	**TRUE.** Residual risk is defined as: "The level of risk that **remains** after management has taken action to mitigate the risk."
28.	A risk Map is a visual depiction of relative risks based on their expected frequency and expected loss.	**TRUE.** A **visual depiction** of relative risks based on their expected frequency and expected loss.
29.	The expected loss is the amount that could likely be lost to the risk event in a very bad year, over the amount budgeted for the expected loss, up to the maximum probable loss. The business should reserve	**FALSE.** The expected loss is the amount that management expects to lose to a given risk per year on average over several years. **Because the loss is expected, it should be included in the budget.**

Muhammad Zain

	the unexpected loss amount as capital.	
30.	The unexpected loss is the largest loss that can occur under foreseeable circumstances. Damage greater than the maximum probable loss could occur, but, in the judgment of management, it is doubtful to occur.	**FALSE.** The amount that could likely be lost to the risk event in a very bad year, in excess of the amount budgeted for the expected loss, up to the **maximum probable loss**. The business should reserve the unexpected loss amount as capital.
31.	The maximum possible loss is the worst-case scenario. It represents the greatest possible loss from a specific risk or event.	**TRUE.** The maximum possible loss is the **worst-case scenario**. It represents the greatest possible loss from a specific risk or event.
32.	Feedforward controls identify a problem after it occurs and attempt to prevent it from occurring.	**FALSE.** Feedforward controls identify a problem **before** it occurs and attempt to prevent it from occurring.
33.	Concurrent controls operate at the same time as the process they monitor and make adjustments	**TRUE. Concurrent controls** operate simultaneously as they monitor and make adjustments based upon immediate feedback from the system.

	based upon immediate feedback from the system.	
34.	Internal controls can provide only limited assurance that objectives can be achieved. Internal controls should never be promoted as a guarantee.	**FALSE.** Internal controls can provide only **reasonable assurance** that objectives can be achieved. Internal controls should never be promoted as a guarantee.
35.	Excessive or unreasonable controls can increase bureaucracy and reduce productivity. Controls must be evaluated in terms of their cost and utility to avoid wasting resources.	**FALSE.** Excessive or unreasonable controls can increase bureaucracy and reduce productivity. Controls must be evaluated in terms of their **cost** and **benefit** to avoid wasting resources.
36.	Virtually all employees are involved in internal control.	**TRUE.** Virtually **all employees** are involved in internal control.
37.	Control Environment is the basic component of Internal Control.	**TRUE.** The control environment **sets the tone** for the organization, influencing the control consciousness of its people. The control environment is the foundation for the other components of internal control.
38.	Control is the result of proper planning, organizing, and	**TRUE.** Control is "any action taken by management, the board, and other parties to enhance risk management and increase the

Muhammad Zain

		likelihood that established objectives and goals will be achieved."
	directing by management.	
39.	Variance analysis is an example of a feedback control	**TRUE.** Feedback controls identify when something has already gone wrong. Variance analysis reviews deviation from a **standard**, so therefore it is feedback control.

SECTION F – FRAUD RISKS (WEIGHTAGE 10%)

STUDY POINTS

S.No	Study Questions	Study Answers
1.	What is **fraud**?	Fraud is defined as "Any illegal act characterized by deceit, concealment, or violation of trust. These acts are not dependent upon the threat of violence or physical force. Frauds are perpetrated by parties and organizations to obtain money, property, or services; to avoid payment or loss of services, or to secure personal or business advantage."
2.	What are the three main **types of fraud**?	The three main types of Fraud are: 1. Fraudulent financial reporting – intentional misstatements, omission of information from financial statements, and misapplication of accounting principles. 2. Misappropriation (theft) of assets – theft, embezzlement, excessive use of company's resources for personal gains. 3. Corruption – bribes, kickbacks, gratuities, etc.
3.	How can fraud **benefit** the **organization**?	The following are examples of fraud that can **benefit the organization**: • Sale or assignment of fictitious or misrepresented assets. • Improper payments, such as illegal political contributions, bribes, kickbacks, and payoffs to government officials, intermediaries of government officials, customers, or suppliers.

		• Intentional, improper representation or valuation of transactions, assets, liabilities, or income. • Intentional, improper transfer pricing (that is, improper valuation of goods exchanged between related organizations). By deliberately structuring pricing techniques improperly, management can improve the operating results of an organization involved in the transaction to the detriment of the other organization. • Intentional, improper related-party transactions in which one party receives some benefit not obtainable to unrelated parties in an arms-length transaction. • Intentional failure to record or disclose significant information to improve the organization's financial picture to outside parties. • Prohibited business activities, such as those that violate government statutes, rules, regulations, or contracts. • Tax fraud.
4.	How can fraud be **detrimental** to the **organization**?	Some examples of fraud that can be **detrimental to the organization** are: • Accepting bribes or kickbacks. • Diverting a potentially profitable transaction that would typically generate profits for the organization to an employee or outsider.

		• Embezzlement or theft, such as misappropriating money or property and falsifying financial records to cover up the act, makes detection difficult. • Intentionally concealing or misrepresenting events or data. • Invoices submitted for services or goods that are not provided to the organization.
5.	What are the **three conditions** necessary for committing **fraud**?	The three conditions necessary for committing fraud are as follows: 1. The person must be **motivated** to commit the fraud. 2. The person must have the **opportunity** to commit the fraud. 3. The person must be able to **rationalize** the fraud. Collectively, these three elements are called the **fraud triangle**. If the company can eliminate any of these three elements, the likelihood of fraud is significantly reduced.
6.	What are the factors that **motivate** the person to commit fraud?	The factors that motivate the person to commit fraud are: • Internal pressure from top management to meet expectations (for example, market or revenue expectations) and not meeting these expectations could lead to job loss or demotion. • External pressure from financers threatens the organization's financial stability (for

		example, not meeting various requirements in a debt agreement). • Pressure to pay for a personal lifestyle or vices (for example, gambling or drugs). • Pressure to maximize performance-based bonuses or compensation (for example, a contingent compensation structure).
7.	What are the factors that **create an opportunity** for a person to commit fraud?	The factors that create an opportunity for a person to commit fraud are: • Knowing the weaknesses in the company's internal control systems. • Poor segregation of duties. • Access to accounting records or assets. • Lack of proper supervision. • Unethical "tone at the top." • A belief that the person will not get caught.
8.	What are the factors that create an **environment to rationalize behaviour** for committing fraud?	The factors that create an environment to rationalize behaviour for committing fraud are: • The individual believes that they have not been correctly financially compensated. Thus, stealing is not stealing; instead, it is another means of getting what is rightfully owed. • The individual believes that they are not getting proper recognition in the workplace. • The individual needs more money.

		• The individual plans to return the stolen money in the future, so the act is equivalent to an interest-free loan.
9.	What is the responsibility of management and the IAA in connection with **fraud**?	**Management** has the responsibility to **establish** and **maintain** an effective control system. The internal auditor is responsible for examining the controls to determine if they are adequate to prevent or detect fraud, as well as looking for occurrences of fraud. However, **the internal auditor is not responsible for preventing fraud.**
10.	What is **management override of controls**?	Override of controls occurs when management overrides or in some way circumvents the controls in place to commit fraud.
11.	What are the **causes** of management fraud?	The causes of management fraud are: • Executives are taking rash steps from which they cannot retreat. • Profit centers distorting facts to hold off divestment. • Incompetent managers are deceiving others to keep their jobs. • Performance distorted to warrant more significant bonuses. • The need to succeed in turning managers to deception.

		• Unscrupulous managers are serving conflicting interests. • Profits inflated to obtain advantages in the marketplace. • The one who controls both the assets and related records is in a position to falsify records.
12.	What are the five key steps of **fraud risk assessment**?	The five steps in fraud risk assessment are as follows: 1. Identify relevant fraud risk factors. 2. Identify potential fraud schemes and prioritize them based on risk. 3. Map existing controls to potential fraud schemes and identify gaps. 4. Test operating effectiveness of fraud prevention and detection controls. 5. Document and report the fraud risk assessment.
13.	What is included in the **Fraud risk assessment**?	• The types of fraud that have some chance of occurring. • The inherent risk of fraud considering the availability of liquid and saleable assets, organizational morale, employee turnover, the history of fraud and losses. • The adequacy of existing anti-fraud programs, monitoring, and preventive controls.

		• The potential gaps in the organization's fraud controls, including segregation of duties. • The likelihood of a significant fraud occurring. • The business impact of fraud.
14.	What **guidance** is provided for auditors conducting Fraud engagements?	• Consider fraud risks in the assessment of internal control design and determination of audit steps to perform. • Have sufficient knowledge of fraud to identify red flags indicating fraud may have been committed. • Be alert to opportunities that could allow fraud, such as control deficiencies. • Evaluate whether management is actively retaining responsibility for oversight of the fraud risk management program. • Evaluate the indicators of fraud. • Recommend investigation when appropriate.
15.	What are **red flags**?	Anything that strongly suggests that an unethical or suspicious event has taken place or is a situation that would enable fraud to occur without detection.
16.	What are **important considerations** relating to red flags?	There are a few essential points to note about red flags: • It is often the case that an auditor will not come across any red flags. However, the

		absence of red flags does not necessarily mean an absence of fraudulent activity. Perpetrators of fraud often skillfully conceal their actions. • Although an auditor might detect a red flag, this does not automatically mean that fraud has been committed. When red flags are identified, the auditor needs to carefully determine if there is an innocent, rational explanation for its presence or if there is a legitimate reason for concern. An area that turns up multiple red flags requires extra attention.
17.	What should the IAA do when there is **reasonable certainty** that a fraud has occurred?	If there is reasonable certainty that fraud has occurred, the CAE should notify the **appropriate management level**, usually the audit committee and perhaps also the board of directors. Management then decides whether or not to start an investigation.
18.	What role should the IAA have in respect to **fraud engagements**?	The specific role of the IAA in a fraud investigation should be outlined in the Charter and possibly in policies and procedures related to fraud. The potential roles for the IAA include: • Leading the investigation, • Being a supporting resource to another party leading the investigation, or • No role at all if the IAA does not have the resources.
19.	When **shall fraud**	If there is reasonable certainty that fraud has occurred, the CAE should notify the **appropriate management level**, usually the

	investigation be started?	audit committee and perhaps also the board of directors. Management then decides whether or not to start an investigation.
		It is generally not the auditor's duty to report fraud to individuals outside of the organization.
20.	What should the IAA do when conducting a **fraud investigation**?	• Assess the probable level and extent of complicity in the fraud within the organization.
		• Determine the knowledge, skills, and other competencies needed to carry out the investigation effectively.
		• Design procedures to identify the perpetrators, the extent of the fraud, the techniques used, and the cause of the fraud.
		• Coordinate activities with management personnel, legal counsel, and other specialists as appropriate throughout the investigation.
		• Be aware of the rights of alleged perpetrators and personnel within the scope of the investigation and the organization's reputation itself.
21.	What should the IAA do after a **fraud investigation**?	• Determine if controls need to be implemented or strengthened.
		• Design engagement tests to help disclose frauds in the future.
		• Maintain sufficient knowledge of fraud to identify future incidents.

22.	What is the **first principle** in *Managing Business Risk Fraud: A Practical Guide*	**Principle 1:** As part of an organization's governance structure, a fraud risk management program should be in place, including a written policy (or policies) to convey the expectations of the board of directors and senior management regarding managing fraud risk.
23.	What is the **second principle** in *Managing Business Risk Fraud: A Practical Guide*	**Principle 2:** Fraud risk exposure should be assessed periodically to identify specific potential schemes and events that the organization needs to mitigate. Ongoing risk management should consider three questions: • How could someone exploit a weakness in the system? • How could someone override or circumvent controls? • How could someone conceal the fraud?
24.	What is the **third principle** in *Managing Business Risk Fraud: A Practical Guide*	**Principle 3:** Prevention techniques to avoid potential key fraud risk events should be established, where feasible, to mitigate possible impacts on the organization. All employees need to be aware of the fraud risk management program to know there is an effort to prevent and detect fraud.
25.	What is the **fourth principle** in *Managing Business Risk Fraud: A Practical Guide*	**Principle 4:** Detection techniques should be established to uncover fraud events when preventive measures fail or unmitigated risks are realized. Detection controls should:

		• Usually be hidden and operate in the background.
		• Be implemented and used in the ordinary course of business.
		• Draw on external information to corroborate internal information.
		• Formally and automatically communicate deficiencies and exceptions to leadership.
		• Use results to enhance and modify other controls.
26.	What is the **fifth principle** in *Managing Business Risk Fraud: A Practical Guide*	**Principle 5**: A reporting process should be in place to solicit input on potential fraud. A coordinated approach to investigation and corrective action should be used to help ensure potential fraud is addressed appropriately and timely.
27.	What is **Whistleblowing**?	Whistleblowing is the act of reporting wrongdoing or suspected wrongdoing outside of the normal chain of command.
28.	What is a key characteristic of a **whistleblowing reporting system**?	To encourage people to share problems, the whistleblowing system needs to be **confidential and anonymous**. It may include a phone number to call or a specific person to contact. It is also possible that a third-party entity may facilitate the whistleblowing process. In addition to setting up such a system, management must ensure that all employees know about it and feel confident that their identities will be protected.

29.	What is **Forensic Auditing**?	When auditing skills are applied to situations that have **potential legal implications** and consequences. Forensic auditing is performed when it has been determined that something inappropriate might have happened, and there is a need to investigate that situation in more depth.
30	What is an **Interrogation**?	In an interrogation, the internal auditor seeks **confirmation** or, ideally, a **confession**. Usually, interrogations are done after evidence has been collected and there is a strong suspicion of fraud or unethical behaviour.
31.	Who performs an **Interrogation**?	At least two people should conduct an interrogation: an experienced individual leads the interrogation, and a second person takes notes and is a corroborating witness. There will most likely be legal counsel involved in both the preparation for the interrogation and its execution to ensure that the company does not place itself at risk of being sued.
32.	What is a **Confession**?	A confession is a complete acknowledgement of wrongdoing by the accused.
33.	What is an **Admission**?	In admission, the accused party acknowledges committing a particular act, but they do not confess that there was the intent, nor does the accused party confess to the accusation.
34.	What are three **common grounds**	1. Defamation of character 2. False imprisonment 3. Malicious prosecution

on which individuals can sue a company that accuses them of Fraud?	

SECTION F – FRAUD RISKS (WEIGHTAGE 10%)

TRUE / FALSE QUESTIONS AND ANSWERS

S.NO	QUESTIONS	ANSWERS
1.	There are three main types of Fraud.	**TRUE.** Fraudulent Financial Reporting, Misappropriation of Assets and Corruption.
2.	There are three conditions necessary for committing fraud	**TRUE.** The person must be **motivated** to commit the fraud. The person must have the **opportunity** to commit the fraud. The person must be able to **rationalize** the fraud.
3.	Management has the responsibility to prevent or detect fraud as well as look for occurrences of fraud.	**FALSE.** The internal auditor is responsible for **examining** the controls to determine if they are adequate to **prevent** or **detect** fraud, as well as looking for occurrences of fraud.
4.	Management has the responsibility to establish and maintain an effective control system.	**TRUE. Management** has the responsibility to **establish** and **maintain** an effective control system.
5.	Override of controls occurs when the board overrides or in some way circumvents the controls in place to commit fraud.	**FALSE.** Override of controls occurs when **management** overrides or in some way circumvents the controls in place to commit fraud.
6.	If there is reasonable certainty that	**FALSE.** If there is reasonable certainty that fraud has occurred, the CAE should notify the **appropriate management level**, usually the

	fraud has occurred, the CAE should apprehend the perpetrator.	audit committee and perhaps also the board of directors. Management then decides whether or not to start an investigation.
7.	The specific role of the IAA in a fraud investigation is not necessary to be outlined in the Charter.	**FALSE.** The specific role of the IAA in a fraud investigation should be **outlined in the Charter** and possibly in policies and procedures related to fraud.
8.	It is generally not the auditor's duty to report fraud to individuals outside of the organization.	**TRUE.** It is generally not the auditor's duty to **report fraud** to individuals **outside** of the organization.
9.	The internal auditor's role involves collecting facts while interviewing an individual during the investigation of suspected fraud.	**TRUE.** The internal auditor mainly **gathers facts** during a fraud investigation.
10.	The internal auditors' responsibility for the prevention of fraud includes ensuring that fraud will not occur.	**FALSE.** The internal auditor's responsibility is to assist in the deterrence of fraud by examining and evaluating the adequacy and effectiveness of the system of internal control. However, internal auditors **cannot ensure that fraud will not occur**.
11.	The Standards gives the internal auditor	**FALSE.** The internal auditor may recommend whatever investigation is considered necessary in the circumstances. Thereafter,

	the authority to investigate fraud.	the auditor should follow up to see that the IAA's responsibilities have been met. Generally, a fraud specialist carries out fraud investigations. **Management** must authorize any internal auditor involvement in an investigation.
12.	An adequate system of internal controls is most likely to detect a fraud perpetrated by a group of employees in collusion.	**FALSE.** An adequate system of internal controls is most likely to detect a fraud perpetrated by a **single employee**. Because of segregation of duties, one employee acting alone may not have the ability to commit fraud; or if one employee were to commit fraud, the chances would be more significant that other employees would detect it.
13.	A key feature distinguishing fraud from other types of crime or impropriety is that fraud always involves the false representation or concealment of a material fact.	**TRUE.** Fraud is something that is done **intentionally**. Fraud is committed when there is false representation or concealment of a material fact.
14.	Authorization of changes to the payroll is both an appropriate personnel function and a deterrent to payroll fraud	**TRUE.** Personnel records comprise an **independent source** of authority for payroll operations such as hiring and termination.
15.	An internal auditor who suspects fraud should	**FALSE.** When an internal auditor suspects fraud, it is recommended that they determine the **possible effects** and discuss the matter

	Interview those who have been involved in the control of assets.	with the **appropriate level of management**, who should then initiate an investigation.
16.	A fraud report is required after the detection phase.	**FALSE.** A written report or other formal communication should be issued after the **investigation phase**. It should include all observations, conclusions, recommendations, and corrective action is taken.
17.	Before issuing a final communication on a fraud investigation, the internal auditor should submit a proposed draft for review by the organization's legal counsel.	**TRUE.** The IAA must evaluate the potential for the occurrence of fraud and how the organization manages fraud risk. It is recommended that a draft of the proposed final communications on fraud should be submitted to **legal counsel for review**. When the internal auditor wants to invoke client privilege, consideration should be given to addressing the report to legal counsel.
18.	In an organization with a separate division primarily responsible for fraud deterrence, the internal audit activity (IAA) examines and evaluates the adequacy and effectiveness of that division's actions taken to deter fraud.	**TRUE.** Internal auditors are responsible for **assisting** in and deterring **fraud** by examining and evaluating the adequacy and the effectiveness of the internal control system, commensurate with the extent of the potential exposure/risk in the various segments of the organization's operations.

19.	Internal auditors are responsible for reporting fraud to senior management and the board when the review of all suspected fraud-related transactions is complete.	**FALSE.** When an internal auditor suspects fraud, they should determine the **possible effects** and discuss the matter with the appropriate level of management, who should then initiate an investigation. However, the internal auditor should have **solid reasons** to suspect that fraud has taken place before reporting it to senior management and the board.
20.	Rapid turnover of the organization's financial executives is an indication of possible fraud	**TRUE.** This is considered a "red flag" that indicates **possible fraud**.
21.	The internal audit activity's responsibility for preventing fraud is to maintain internal control.	**FALSE.** Control is the principal means of preventing fraud. **Management**, in turn, is primarily **responsible** for the **establishment and maintenance of control**. In an assurance engagement, internal auditors are primarily responsible for preventing fraud by examining and evaluating the adequacy and effectiveness of control.

BOOKS WRITTEN BY MUHAMMAD ZAIN

List of Books Published since February 2017:

1. CIA Part 1 Essentials of Internal Auditing 2022 (21 October 2021)
    Web: https://zainacademy.us/product/cia-part-1-essentials-of-internal-auditing-2022/
    Web: https://mzain.org/cia-part-1-esssentials-of-internal-auditing-2022/

2. CIA Part 3 Business Knowledge for Internal Auditing 2022 (11 October 2021)
    Web: https://zainacademy.us/product/cia-part-3-business-knowledge-for-internal-auditing-2022/
    Web: https://mzain.org/cia-part-3-business-knowledge-for-internal-auditing-2022/

3. CIA Test Bank Questions 2022 (13 September 2021)
    Web: https://zainacademy.us/product/cia-test-bank-questions-2022/
    Web: https://mzain.org/cia-test-bank-questions-2022/

4. CIA Part 3 Test Bank Questions 2022 (09 September 2021)
    Web: https://zainacademy.us/product/cia-part-3-test-bank-questions-2022/
    Web: https://mzain.org/cia-part-3-test-bank-questions-2022/

5. CIA Challenge Exam Test Bank Questions 2022 (06 September 2021)
    Web: https://zainacademy.us/product/cia-challenge-exam-test-bank-questions-2022/
    Web: https://mzain.org/cia-challenge-exam-test-bank-questions-2022/

6. CIA Part 2 Test Bank Questions 2022 (26 August 2021)
    Web: https://zainacademy.us/product/cia-part-2-test-bank-questions-2022/
    Web: https://mzain.org/cia-part-2-test-bank-questions-2022/

7. CIA Part 1 Test Bank Questions 2022 (16 August 2021)
   Web: https://zainacademy.us/product/cia-part-1-test-bank-questions-2022/
   Web: https://mzain.org/cia-part-1-test-bank-questions-2022/

8. CPA Auditing and Attestation 2021 (26 July 2021)
   Web: https://zainacademy.us/product/cpa-auditing-and-attestation-2021/
   Web: https://mzain.org/cpa-auditing-and-attestation-2021/

9. CIA Review Complete 2021 (15 June 2021)
   Web: https://zainacademy.us/product/cia-review-complete-2021/
   Web: https://mzain.org/cia-review-complete-2021/

10. CIA Part 2 Practice of Internal Auditing 2021 (05 May 2021)
    Web: https://zainacademy.us/product/cia-part-2-practice-of-internal-auditing-2021/
    Web: https://mzain.org/cia-part-2-practice-of-internal-auditing-2021/

11. CIA Challenge Exam Study Book 2021 (03 May 2021)
    Web: https://zainacademy.us/product/cia-challenge-exam-study-book-2021/
    Web: https://mzain.org/cia-challenge-exam-study-book-2021/

12. CIA Part 1 Essentials of Internal Auditing 2021 (23 April 2021)
    Web: https://zainacademy.us/product/cia-part-1-essentials-of-internal-auditing-2021/
    Web: https://mzain.org/cia-part-1-essentials-of-internal-auditing-2021/

13. CIA Part 3 Business Knowledge for Internal Auditing 2021 (14 April 2021)
    Web: https://zainacademy.us/product/cia-part-3-2021/
    Web: https://mzain.org/cia-part-3-business-knowledge-for-internal-auditing-2021/

14. CMA Preparation Pack 2021 (24 March 2021)
    Web: https://zainacademy.us/product/cma-preparation-pack-2021/
    Web: https://mzain.org/cma-preparation-pack-2021/

15. CMA Part 1 Preparation Pack 2021 (22 March 2021)
    Web: https://zainacademy.us/product/cma-part-1-preparation-pack-2021/
    Web: https://mzain.org/cma-part-1-preparation-pack-2021/

16. CMA Part 2 Preparation Pack 2021 (12 February 2021)
    Web: https://zainacademy.us/product/cma-part-2-preparation-pack-2021/
    Web: https://mzain.org/cma-part-2-preparation-pack-2021/

17. CIA Challenge Exam Test Bank Questions 2021 (26 November 2020)
    Web: https://zainacademy.us/product/cia-challenge-exam-2021/
    Web: https://mzain.org/cia-challenge-exam-2021/

18. CIA Part 3 Test Bank Questions 2021 (22 November 2020)
    Web: https://zainacademy.us/product/cia-part-3-test-bank-questions-2021/
    Web: https://mzain.org/cia-part-3-test-bank-questions-2021/

19. CIA Part 1 Test Bank Questions 2021 (28 September 2020)
    Web: https://zainacademy.us/product/cia-part-1-test-bank-questions-2021/
    Web: https://mzain.org/cia-part-1-test-bank-questions-2021/

20. CIA Part 2 Test Bank Questions 2021 (10 September 2020)
Web: https://zainacademy.us/product/cia-part-2-test-bank-2021/
Web: https://mzain.org/cia-part-2-test-bank-questions-2021/

21. CMA Part 2 Strategic Financial Management 2020 (21 April 2020)
Web: https://zainacademy.us/product/cma-part-2-2020/
Web: https://mzain.org/cma-part-2-strategic-financial-management-2020/

22. CMA Part 1 Financial Planning, Performance and Analytics 2020 (01 February 2020)
Web: https://zainacademy.us/product/cma-part-1-study-book-2020/
Web: https://mzain.org/cma-part-1-financial-planning-performance-and-analytics-2020/

23. CIA Part 2 Test Bank Questions 2020 (24 December 2019)
Web: https://zainacademy.us/product/cia-part-2-test-bank-2020/
Web: https://mzain.org/cia-part-2-test-bank-questions-2020/

24. CIA Part 3 Test Bank Questions 2020 (14 December 2019)
Web: https://zainacademy.us/product/cia-part-3-test-bank-2020/
Web: https://mzain.org/cia-part-3-test-bank-questions-2020/

25. CIA Part 1 Test Bank Questions 2020 (08 December 2019)
Web: https://zainacademy.us/product/cia-part-1-test-bank-2020/
Web: https://mzain.org/cia-part-1-test-bank-questions-2020/

26. CIA Part 2 Practice of Internal Auditing 2020 (25 September 2019)
Web: https://zainacademy.us/product/cia-part-2-2020/
Web: https://mzain.org/cia-part-2-practice-of-internal-auditing-2020/

27. CIA Part 1 Essentials of Internal Auditing 2020 (12 September 2019)
    Web: https://zainacademy.us/product/cia-part-1-2020/
    Web: https://mzain.org/cia-part-1-essentials-of-internal-auditing-2020/

28. CPA Business Environment and Concepts (BEC) 2019 (22 July 2019)
    Web: https://zainacademy.us/product/cpa-business-environment-and-concepts-bec-2019/
    Web: https://mzain.org/cpa-business-environment-and-concepts-bec-2019/

29. CIA Part 2 Practice of Internal Auditing 2019 (11 April 2019)
    Web: https://zainacademy.us/product/cia-part-2-practice-of-internal-auditing-2019/
    Web: https://mzain.org/cia-part-2-practice-of-internal-auditing-2019/

30.   CIA Part 1 Essentials of Internal Auditing 2019 (17 February 2019)
    Web: https://zainacademy.us/product/cia-part-1-essentials-of-internal-auditing-2019/
    Web: https://mzain.org/cia-part-1-essentials-of-internal-auditing-2019/

31. CIA Part 3 Business Knowledge for Internal Auditing 2019 (05 January 2019)
    Web: https://zainacademy.us/product/cia-part-3-business-knowledge-for-internal-auditing-2019/
    Web: https://mzain.org/cia-part-3-business-knowledge-for-internal-auditing-2019/

32. Certified Management Accountant (CMA) – Part 1 – 2019 (07 October 2018)
Web: https://zainacademy.us/product/cma-part-1-financial-reporting-planning-performance-and-control-2019/
Web: https://mzain.org/cma-part-1-financial-reporting-planning-performance-and-control-2019/

33. Certified Management Accountant (CMA) – Part 2 – 2019 (13 September 2018)
Web: https://zainacademy.us/product/cma-part-2-financial-decision-making-2019/
Web: https://mzain.org/cma-part-2-financial-decision-making-2019/

QUOTES THAT WILL CHANGE YOUR LIFE

These are the quotes that have made what I am today. You can also be the one in your Universe:

- We are born in one day. We die in one day. We can change in one day. And we can fall in love in one day Anything can happen in just one day.

- The finest of the brains are in extreme level of slavery. For them, career and job are important than financial freedom and peace of soul. You will be replaced in a day or two when you leave this world for eternal life. Not understanding this point will lead to a dead end tunnel. Seek certification to change your world, wellbeing and most important yourself.

- Excellence, Creativity, Passion, and Patience are key ingredients to become a Star.

- Get up and Hustle. Chase your dreams. Turn your dreams into reality by showing up every day.

- Have Confidence. You can do it. You have the capacity and potential to reach the top. Just believe in your abilities and chase your dream.

- Dream is what seen by an open eye, not with the closed one.

- Dreams don't work unless you do.

- What we learn becomes a part of who we are.

- The right way to start your day is to focus on end goal.

- Sometimes the bad things that happen in our lives put us directly on the path to the best things that will ever happen to us.

- A creative man is motivated by the desire to achieve, not by the desire to beat others.

- Twenty years from now you will be more disappointed by the things that you didn't do than by the ones you did do. So throw off the bowlines. Sail away from the safe harbor. Catch the trade winds in your sails. Explore. Dream. Discover.

- It does not matter how slow you go. So long as you don't stop.

- It is never too late to begin.

- If it scares you, it might be a good thing to try.

- There is only you and your camera. The limitations in your photography are in yourself, for what we see is what we are.

- Creativity is Intelligence having fun.

- All progress takes place out of comfort zone, so when are you starting.

- Everything you have ever wanted is on the other side of fear.

- When everything seems to be going against you, remember that the airplane takes off against the wind, not with it.

- Unexpected kindness is the most powerful, least costly, and most underrated agent of human change.

- Sometimes courage is the quiet voice at the end of the day saying I will try again tomorrow.

- Sometimes you win, sometimes you learn.

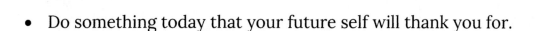

- Do something today that your future self will thank you for.

- The past has no power over the present moment. So forget about your failures and start a new day.

- Most of the important things in the world have been accomplished by people who have kept on trying when there seemed to be no help at all.

- Your imagination is everything. It is the preview of life's coming attractions. Only those who believe anything is possible can achieve things most would consider impossible.

- Don't let the noise of others' opinions drown out your own inner voice.

- Have the courage to follow your heart and intuition. They somehow already know what you truly want to become. Everything else is secondary.

- Your time is limited, so don't waste it living someone else's life.

- Remembering that you are going to die is the best way I know to avoid the trap of thinking you have something to lose. You are already naked. There is no reason not to follow your heart.

- Your work is going to fill large part of your life and the only way to be truly satisfied is to do what you believe is great work. The only way to do great work is to love what you do. If you haven't found it yet, keep looking. Don't settle. As with all matters of the heart, you will know when you find it.

- Success doesn't come from what you do occasionally. It comes from what you do consistently.

- If opportunity doesn't knock, build a door.

Muhammad Zain

- The things you regret most in life are the risks you didn't take.

- Every successful person was once an unknown person that refused to give up on their dream.

- Life is too short to be working for someone else's dream.

- It always seems impossible until it's done.

- Innovation distinguishes between a leader and a follower.

- Success is not final; failure is not fatal. It is the courage to continue that counts.

- Every problem is a gift. Without problems, we would not grow.

- There is no shortage of remarkable ideas, what's missing is the will to execute them.

- Forget past mistakes. Forget failures. Forget everything except what you are going to do now and do it.

- Many of life's failure are people who did not realize how close they were to success when they gave up.

- If something is important enough, or you believe something is important enough, even if you are scared, you will keep going.

- The best way to predict the future is to create it.

- The only strategy that is guaranteed to fail is not taking risks.

- Only those who will risk going too far can possibly find out how far one can go.

- Don't waste words on people who deserve your silence. Sometimes the most powerful thing you can say is nothing at all.

Muhammad Zain

Made in the USA
Las Vegas, NV
10 December 2023

82508035R00105